A LIFE ON THE LINES

THE GRAND OLD MAN OF STEAM

SECOND EDITION

A LIFE ON THE LINES

THE GRAND OLD MAN OF STEAM

SECOND EDITION

RHN HARDY

CONWAY

BLOOMSBURY

LONDON · NEW DELHI · NEW YORK · SYDNEY

AUTHOR'S ACKNOWLEDGEMENTS

I would like to thank Bloomsbury Publishing who have taken over the publishing of this second edition of the book and in particular publisher, Janet Murphy and editor, Jonathan Eyers. I owe a particular debt to Rupert Wheeler whose idea this book was and whose judgement has helped me so much in bringing this book together. I must also thank both Philip Murgatroyd and Ben Maclay (as well as my own family), who have forgotten more than I shall ever know about computers and their little ways. Had it not been for their practical support, I should have got nowhere very fast indeed. And finally my gratitude to Barry Hoper for the excellent printing of my old box camera negatives and the work of the Transport Treasury who have made those images available worldwide and to the descendants of men whose photographs I took at work maybe over 70 years ago.

Conway
An imprint of Bloomsbury Publishing Plc

50 Bedford Square
London
WC1B 3DP
UK

1385 Broadway
New York
NY 10018
USA

ISBN: HB: 978-1-8448-6335-8
ePDF: 978-18448-6430-0
ePub: 978-1-8448-6431-7

2 4 6 8 10 9 7 5 3 1

www.bloomsbury.com

First published by Anova Books Ltd 2012
Second edition published by Bloomsbury 2016

British Library Cataloguing-in-Publication Data
A catalogue record for this book is available from the British Library.

Library of Congress Cataloguing-in-Publication data has been applied for.

Typeset in MetaPlus Book 9 on 11pt by Posthouse Publishing Ltd
Printed and bound in China by C&C Offset Printing Co

Bloomsbury Publishing Plc makes every effort to ensure that the papers used in the manufacture of our books are natural, recyclable products made from wood grown in well managed forests. Our manufacturing processes conform to the environmental regulation of the country of origin.

To find out more about our authors and books visit www.bloomsbury.com. Here you will find extracts, author interviews, details of forthcoming events and the option to sign up for our newsletters.

All images are the copyright of The Transport Treasury (www.transporttreasury.co.uk) apart from those listed separately below. The majority of Transport Treasury photographs were taken by the author, but photographs by A E Bennett, R C Riley, R E Vincent, Dr I C Allen and G A Barlow have also been included.
Nick Brodrick 6, Andrew Dow front cover and 29 top left, Peter Hardy 189, David Kindred 1, 90 & 105 , Trevor Tupper 177, Adrian Vaughan 85 far right, 96, 97 bottom right. Antony Guppy 177, Barry Hoper 183.
National Railway Museum / Science & Society Picture Library 29 bottom right, 31 top, 32 all images, 38 all images, 41, 46 top left and bottom left, 49 top and bottom right, 50 left, 51 right, 53 all images, 57, 58 both images, 61, 65 bottom right, 70, 72, 85, 92, 95 right, 9 right, 125 bottom left, 129, 137, 138 left, 141 right, 169 both images and 187 John Sagar.

CONTENTS

INTRODUCTION

ABOVE: I retired as Chairman of the Steam Locomotive Association (SLOA) in 1993 and the committee organised a special train to Dover Marine and back to Victoria. The train was hauled by No 70000 *Britannia* masquerading as *William Shakespeare* No 70004. However, the engine that arrived in Dover was a light engine from Stewarts Lane and bore the name John Peck on one side and Richard Hardy on the other. John had been Chief Mechanical Engineer of SLOA for the same six years as me and both of us had been professional railwaymen. The Britannia Society gave me the nameplate which now rests against the fireplace.

LEFT: In the cab of *Oliver Cromwell* at Colchester.

TOP FAR LEFT AND RIGHT: These are taken with the old box camera about 1957–8 at Stewarts Lane in the cab of a Fairbairn 'Midland' tank. For my children, James and Anthea, it was a bi-annual treat to come down on a Sunday morning to Stewarts Lane shed long after I had moved on to Stratford. They always had the shop officeman, Syd Norman, as their guide, who amused them when they had had their fill of getting on to engines in the shed.

FAR LEFT BOTTOM: A classic family photograph of Bert Hooker and my son Peter in the cab of No 73082 at Waterloo before Bert left for Salisbury. It was every little boy's desire to be an engine driver in those days, although this picture was taken in about 1960 and the interest in steam traction was beginning to wane.

In July 1936 when I was 12, rising 13, my parents gave me a Kodak Box camera just before we went on holiday to Lausanne overlooking Lake Geneva: the idea was that I should take an educational interest in my surroundings and so I did to the extent of three scenic efforts with the camera, two of the Lausanne trams and about 20 pictures of the splendid paddle steamers on Lac Leman. Their engines and their shaven-headed engineers were visible for all to see but actually I loved every moment of that holiday and in 1949, on our honeymoon, my wife and I stayed at the same hotel and travelled in the same paddle-steamers. But the day before I left, there was just time to visit Amersham station on the 'Metropolitan and Great Central (Met & GC) and photograph the arrival of the 1606 to Marylebone.

The engine was a Great Central Director No 5506 Butler-Henderson and although my first photograph was quite good with the train slowing up to stop, the second included the driver who turned out to be Fred France, who fired the engine of the first train to leave Marylebone in 1899. He was then a Gorton fireman but came south to Neasden in 1902 as a driver, retiring in 1937 at the age of 65, no doubt without a railway pension. In time, I developed an understanding of what it meant to be a railwayman, a booking clerk, a signalman, a porter, the ganger and his trackmen, an engine driver or a fireman. On the stationmaster's half-day, I was allowed into the signal-box for instruction and I was taken on the footplate to Aylesbury or Rickmansworth, boarding in a cloud of steam to avoid being seen. Arthur Ross, in 1939 a 40 year old fireman at Neasden, wrote to me answering my questions and Ted Simpson, who retired three months after I started on the railway, wrote to me at school inviting me to travel on the engine of the Night Mail from Marylebone to Aylesbury. I carried that letter wherever I went and longed for the usual GC Caprotti but, on the night, it was the newly arrived *Woolwinder No 2554*, an A1 Pacific which suited our driver who was already a Gresley convert!

My parents encouraged me as can be seen from my 'Engine Driver' photograph. In 1929, I was given a copy of *The Railway Magazine* and this monthly gift until the end of 1940 was of immeasurable value. But when I started as a Premium Apprentice at Doncaster Plant Works in Jan 1941, I was paid 16 shillings and tuppence a week (about 80p) and my digs were 30 shillings – so that was the end of my railway magazine!

By Christmas 1936, I had saved up over many months and bought the *British Steam Locomotive 1825–1925* by E L Ahrons, a magnificent treatise. I spent a few wonderful days in March 1931 with the parents of a dear family friend in Mexborough: a visit to the engine sheds at Mexborough and Doncaster, a visit to Manvers main colliery, a glass blowing factory and a short trip with the driver of a 'Trackless Tram.' I was meeting much older people whose life revolved around the railway and how I loved to listen to them.

My mother was widowed in 1938 and she had a struggle with the school fees and was delighted when I left school and entered the 'Doncaster University of Life,' hard but so very rewarding in one's understanding of life and above all, of one's fellow human beings. I was not an academic but the change from a tough but happy life at boarding school to the rigours of B Shop in wartime was not difficult for I was accepted immediately, not only by the older men but more surprisingly by the mature craft apprentices of 15 year olds (in their second year) who were to start my education. The foreman marched me down the shop and its banks of lathes and put me with a certain Denis Branton who was working a turret-lathe. "Hello, kiddo," says Denis, "and what do they call you?" "Richard," I replied and he laughed. "No, you're Dick," and so I was for the rest of my time on the railway. "You speak a bit queer, Dick, you must come from London." "Not far away," I said and Denis said he had never been there: nor had maybe 60 per cent of the work force in the days of only one week's holiday a year in Leger week! My boots were nipping my feet after a week or two of endless standing so, on Denis' advice, I bought a pair of clogs which cost 8/6 a pair whereupon I became 'Cloggy Dick.' Wonderful working footwear, warm, tireless and safe.

Now the major purpose of this work is to show you some of my photographs taken during the war when films were unobtainable and photography mostly forbidden. I owe a particular debt to Rupert Wheeler whose idea it was to put this book together and whose judgement has helped me so much. My negatives now belong to Barry Hoper's Transport Treasury so that my old negatives, lost for many years, are now in safe hands and available on the their website all over

TOP LEFT: This is the second photo I took with my Box Brownie 620 in August 1936 of D11 No 5506 *Butler Henderson* at Amersham of the 4:06pm to Marylebone, all stations Leicester – Harrow-on-the-Hill and fast to Marylebone.

Driver Fred France, who retired in 1937, fired on the first train out of Marylebone in 1899 to Driver Ernie Grain. You can see him on the fireman's side of that famous 'aerial' photo where the bigshots are congregated round the engine and Ernie Grain is standing at the regulator in frock coat and pot hat. Fred was driving expresses before the 1914–18 war and was moved from Gorton to Neasden in the early years of the 20th century.

TOP RIGHT: Taken in 1929 on the front doorstep of his home in Leatherhead, is a certain Richard Hardy probably nearing six years of age. I had been invited to a fancy-dress party and my mother had decided that I should go as an engine-driver. But how did one find out how engine drivers dressed at work? My mother went to see the stationmaster who took her along the track to talk to the driver-in-charge of the Drummond 700 class engine that was shunting the yard.

So there you have me holding an engineman's oil-feeder donated by the driver as well as the sponge-cloth sticking out of my right hand pocket.

BOTTOM: One of my favourite box camera photos on a Sunday morning in July 1939 from Hyrons Lane bridge south of Amersham and where the gradient eases from 1 in 105 after the bridge. Each Sunday in 1939 excursions ran to Sheffield, Nottingham and, I think, to Derby Friargate at 9:50, 10:00 and 10:05am ex Marylebone. They were usually ten coaches or more and I never saw one hauled by other than a B3 4-cylinder, almost invariably Nos 6166, 6167 and 6168, all Caprotti engines and very good indeed for the job. *Valour*, 6165, also worked one of the trains from time to time. Here, No 6168 *Lord Stuart of Wortley* is climbing the last stretch of the bank on the point of blowing off steam and the fireman has put a good poultice in there to last him until he starts to climb up to Dutchlands, the next summit.

the world which is just what I wanted. Over the years Real Photographs and Tim Shuttleworth had done a wonderful job of printing for my albums but I knew that as my railway photographs, with only a few exceptions, included people standing in front of or on an engine, they might not appeal to all collectors of locomotive photographs. So you will find that some 50 of the 120 excellent enlargements by Barry Hoper date back to 1941–45 and they are largely of men who went out of their way to befriend me and teach me and make life truly happy for me. As more than one West Riding engineman said: "Dick, one day you are going to be a boss. You come with us and we'll teach you all we know for if you don't know our job inside out, you'll be neither use nor bloody ornament to us or anybody else."

I had no footplate pass and those men had nothing to gain from their kindness but my gratitude and the knowledge that they were shaping my life. I was never going to be a Chief Mechanical Engineer nor could I contemplate being a designer nor a Works Manager for I was but a very ordinary engineer. But I was going to build my life in the Locomotive Running Department with all its infinite variety and excitement and its close proximity to those thousands of very independent and able men who actually ran the railway.

And so to my little box camera which did a great job but took a battering and by 1946 was not to be relied on so I bought another for 5 shillings and after my mother died, I found hers, another Box which served me well until Dick Riley made me lash out with a Zeiss Nettar at £11 in 1959! So I haven't troubled you with any photographs of the 5 shillings era whereas in the War, the lady in Bagshaws, the photography shop in St Sepulchre Gate, Doncaster, would let this filthy apparition of a boy in overalls have a 620 film with 8 on a spool in the knowledge that he would reappear by and by and place an order for a few prints, some of which made it down the years in family albums. That lady was marvellous and the negatives, which were lost in one of our moves, were found again when I was moved up to Liverpool in 1968. So I was able to have the best enlarged to postcard size in 1969 and create an album where each picture tells a story and which is now a social history of life 70 years ago where people mostly lived very hard and yet were endlessly friendly towards 'Young Dick.' So there will be plenty from that period for men loved to have their photograph taken, as did our lady labourer Phoebe Cliff when I was in the Crimpsall. When I took enginemen, we were usually in a yard or at a station platform, not often in a shed until I was given a footplate pass in 1944 which I hung on to until, in my first job, in July 1945 at Stratford, I was under the great L P Parker who made you ride on engines wherever you went!

LEFT: No 4556 was one of the Leeds superheated N1s, the other being No 4592. For the record, other superheaters were No 4572 at Ardsley; and Nos 4557, 4584, 4598, 4599, 4602 and 4603 at Bradford – splendid engines and very well liked, as were the saturated N1s. The N2s, which left in 1941 after the Bramley derailment, were quick in the uptake and strong but would not steam freely without some unauthorised additions across the blastpipe. There were no tears shed when the unwanted and top-heavy N2s went away to be foisted on some other shed. Taken outside Leeds Central station: Driver Ernest Hine, ex GC Barnsley Junction (Penistone), a cheerful, good-hearted man and Fireman Wilf Webster, the elder of the two brothers, very broad of speech and wearing a splendid pair of clogs. Brother Arthur wore clogs until he retired deep in the diesel age.

In January 1946, I was a Supernumerary Foreman at King's Lynn and then acted as shedmaster at South Lynn for a total of fourteen months until 1948 and after a spell in Mr Parker's 'House of Correction', Motive Power HQ at Liverpool St, he appointed me firstly as shedmaster Woodford, then Ipswich and then before I was 29, he engineered my move to Stewarts Lane, Battersea, a year before he retired in 1953. It was his intention to set things up for my return and his successor brought me back to the Stratford District as Assistant District Motive Power Superintendent (DMPS) in January 1955.

Now I felt that it was not the thing when I was the guv'nor either of a depot or later a district to walk about with a camera and taking pot shots here and there. I thought it was bad for discipline and I was right but there were plenty of visiting photographers like Doctor Ian Allen to whom we gave Dick Elmer, the Stratford Inspector, as a guide who used to say "I wonder where Doctor Allen will take me today." However, I was never allowed to see the photograph that Ian took inside the famous Stratford coaling plant. How he got to his vantage point above the bunkers and the chutes, I do not know and I have never enquired! But the photograph will be reproduced here, a remarkable vantage point and you will be able to see the fascinating view and see for yourselves how Doctor Allen and Inspector Dick Elmer bent the safety rules of today and maybe those days, come to that! But in the collection at the Transport Treasury, there are many pictures of our men either at work or posing for photographs taken by the likes of Ian or Dick Riley or Roy Vincent.

I might have arranged this but I didn't take the photographs which made all the difference! But that means you have a gap of quite a few years in my own collection which we have managed to bridge and later on add to with press photographs which found their way into my album. You will also see Transport Treasury photographs with short captions selected by me at Rupert's request which do not include railwaymen but which have a special relevance or interest.

I have tried to make the point that railwaymen of all sorts are central to the business of running a railway. I had some tough times especially in my earlier days on the Southern at that marvellous depot at Stewarts Lane but at the end of a year, I knew every man in the place whether he was a labourer, chargehand fitter, clerk, boiler washer, stores issuer or engineman. I knew a great deal about his ability to do his job and his personality but not about his home life unless our help was truly needed: but there were still quite a few little dodges I had not rumbled, as the present day survivors are delighted to tell me when we meet at

RIGHT: Leeds Central with a Lanky man on a Midland Compound No 1185 in the background and keeping an eye on us LNER tykes. Driver Herbert Pollard, now a passed fireman and who had fired for Burridge on No 4460 on the Pullman jobs before 1937 when the Pacifics, Nos 2553/5 arrived for the *Queen of Scots*. Herbert had a quiet voice and was known as the 'Whispering Baritone'. Tim Paley and Stan Hodgson both in the second tankie gang, No 3 Link. Tim is eating an apple and Stan smoking a rare pipe. Stan was the man who started it all for me in the West Riding that night he invited me on to the footplate of No 6100, B4 at Wakefield to ride to Doncaster with him and Bob Foster. He had started at the end of December 1922 and was, in 1941, still a 'Young Hand'. But he was an extrovert and asked me, a scruffy boy of 17 looking into the cab at Wakefield Kirkgate, who I was and where I was going and he and Bob put me through my first lesson in preparation and disposal in the early hours in the Garden Sidings before returning to Leeds. And, of course, he was proud of being a Great Northern man if only by two days service!

our little gatherings, for it is 60 years since I first went 'Dahn the Lane.' There is one more point that I should make: many of us Eastern and Southern folk never grasped the need for shed plates and their codes nor did we use the extra 3 or 6 ahead of the regional number except with the Bulleid Pacifics and the 'Charleys'. I am sure that you will understand that it would be quite unnatural for me, in this sort of book, to adopt what amounts to an unnatural house-style. As for shed codes, all I can say is that I was DMPS at Liverpool St for four years and the Assistant before that and when in recent years, I had to include the Southend code in a piece of writing, I had to apply to David Butcher, meticulous author, friend and one-time fireman at Southend, who told me it was 30D but for the life of me, I still don't know the whereabouts of 30B, C, E, F and G although I have a shrewd idea that Stratford was 30A.

Here are two short stories to finish. Stan Hinbest started at Stratford Running Sheds in 1944 as an apprentice fitter and we first met the following year when I went there to chase material to keep engines at work in those difficult times. Stan worked in the machine shop and I worked closely with his Chargehand, Jack Welsh, which did not stop that young man burrowing, late one afternoon, under the wide bench on which I was doing some paperwork, with a pot of whitewash and skilfully decorating my shoes! There was much laughter in which I joined but it was over 45 years before the artist himself let on! Stan was skinny and small and it was no surprise when Fred Lucas, the Foreman came into the shop, spotted Stan and said: "I've a little job for you, son, come along with me."

It seemed to Stan that fat men always got the job of taking out the regulator in the dome and of undoing the four bolts that held the regulator casting to the main steam-pipe. There were also the two pins further down which were held in position by split pins, to provide the linkage between the regulator and the spindle that went through to the cab. How easy this may sound if the nuts and pins came free easily but they never did for Stan when he had been lowered head first into the dome with the lower part of his midriff and his legs still outside and his arms at full stretch holding a hammer, chisel, spanner and maybe a pin-punch. If the nuts on the bolts defied every effort to free them, they had to be chopped off with the hammer and chisel, bad enough right-way up but far worse for a 14 year old upside down with his arms at full stretch.

But the job always got done, often with a bruised left hand when the hammer missed the chisel but the main thing Stan had to learn was to empty his top pocket as his cigarettes and lighter would soon disappear into the boiler, never to

LEFT: Here are two ladies standing against No 4771 *Green Arrow*. They are standing on the ballast, well off the platform at Stratford-on-Avon, as are several other would-be passengers and photographers in the days before Health and Safety. My wife Gwenda is on the right with her lifelong friend Pat Carden. They had come to Stratford from High Wycombe behind No 4771 to soak up the culture, whereas I had come to work my passage.

The photograph was taken in 1991 in the days when sensible photographers were allowed to take photographs such as these. You can see a couple in action and good luck to them as such a picture could never be taken today.

In the first 24 years of our marriage Gwenda and I moved home seven times, which made life very difficult, but it was the same for most railway officers who had to move for promotion and in fact it increased one's experience immensely. But from 1973 onwards, we never had to move again and Gwenda said when I retired in 1982, "This is where we are going to stay!" And so we made our home in Amersham.

return, followed sometimes by one of the fitter's spanners, for the loss of which he would receive a cuff round the ear! As Stan said: "That's one of the pitfalls of being a small and thin apprentice." But after seven years of hard work, he was a real craftsman.

In March 1953, our Chief Clerk, Charlie Bayliss, at Stewarts Lane asked me to interview a potential engine cleaner, several years older than the usual school leavers of the day. Charles said that he was something special and so he was. He was very dark skinned, mature and immediately likeable and I could see that Charles was right. So Percy Abeydeera from Ceylon started on the railway and achieved his aim to become an engine-driver in this country. We did not have many boys from abroad at that time, four from the West Indies, two from Africa and Michael Motha from Sri Lanka who was doing well as a young fireman.

We had some good cleaners at that time on the verge of being appointed firemen so Percy began to go firing but when there was a special job which demanded a very high level of cleanliness, we used him and one or two regulars of his seniority. So it was that Percy helped to clean the Schools class, 915 for the Queen's journey from Victoria to Tattenham Corner for the Derby. And then in the autumn of 1954, Haile Selassie, Emperor of Abyssinia, visited this country and was welcomed by the Queen at Victoria station. The engine was No 34088, one of our Bulleids, and she looked a picture when she went off to Eastleigh light engine ready for our men to bring the Royal Train up from Gosport next day.

Percy had worked wonders on that engine along with his fellow cleaners and adult helpers and, when the Emperor returned a few weeks later, I took Percy over to Victoria on No 34088 to see the young Queen Elizabeth and the Prime Minister, the legendary Winston Churchill. But also to witness the departure of Stewarts Lane's handiwork and its gentle, smooth and all but silent start from Victoria, something that Percy could treasure down the years. Driver George (Honey) King was in charge with Syd Hudson as his stoker.

It has given me great pleasure to keep in touch with Percy and, well after I left the Lane in January 1955, I was able to give him experience of footplate work with Stratford men to Ipswich and wherever he went amongst locomen, he was welcomed. In time he had married a Swiss lady and when he retired, he invited Gwenda and me to dine with the Abeydeera family at an ASLEF gathering, a happy evening surrounded by his old mates from the Lane. In time, he lost his wife and he faced life with great fortitude, an example to all of us. He undertakes all manner of handy work for friends and family, he goes to railway gatherings and

RIGHT: Stewarts Lane in 1957, more than two years after I had left the Lane in January 1955. This Brighton Atlantic No 2424 was by all accounts a wonderful engine for her age. The last Great Northern C1 from which the Brighton engines were derived, had been withdrawn in 1951: what No 2424 was doing at The Lane, one can only guess although the photograph has two Stewarts Lane fitters and two fitters mates and one shop officeman. The Fitter on the left is Art Martin, a man of experience and I think he originated from the Battersea Park depot and came over to Stewarts Lane when the shed was closed in 1933. Les Penfold on the right is his quiet and knowledgeable mate, and in the centre is Sid Norman.

FAR RIGHT TOP: This elderly driver looks the part and yet he has fallen on hard times and has had to come off the footplate for some good reason, maybe eyesight or the dreaded colour vision. He may be a cloth cap man or just refuses to wear the LMS shiny top pattern which has become standard. The photograph is marked Doncaster so we must be in the early 50s.

FAR RIGHT BOTTOM: A little Great Eastern J69, No 8499, had been built in 1890 and lasted to the end of steam at Stratford in September 1962. She had been many years in Scotland having been transferred there in about 1927. She and several others returned to Stratford in the mid-1950s. Here you see No 8499 at Stratford by no means smart and requiring the excellent services of the young Stan Hinbest, one of the 'Westo' tankside fitters in the Jubilee shed. It is difficult to see what Stan is doing and his foot on the running board looks a bit precarious and certainly he and all his mates never heard of 'H&S'.

not long ago with other Stewarts Lane men, he visited the Keighley and Worth Valley Railway and there was old No 34092 well on its way to the completion of an extensive general repair, an engine he often fired when he was with Driver Cecil Dudley. But he also travels the world to see his very old friends. Not long ago, I received a card from West Bengal to say that he had been to Darjeeling 'to see and go on the steam engine!' Now in his early 80s, he will soon be back and at our next gathering. But what an example of the 'Great Brotherhood of Railwayman' that binds us all together, of our men who cared nothing for colour and far more for a young man who was willing to learn and be friendly to all. That was Percy and his friend from Ceylon, Michael Motha.

LEFT: This photograph was published in the March 1940 *Railway Magazine* and the B12 is having a very rough time, brought about by 'engine priming bad' as I once saw written by a driver on the Southend repair sheet in 1945. Somebody had had a rough trip with priming and their engine needed a washout or perhaps the fireman had been over-eager: we shall never know. But here is No 8577, one of the last of the B12s to be built, tackling the 1 in 58 from Saxmundham Junction towards Leiston.

She has been standing for 20 minutes, waiting for a train to come off the Aldeburgh branch and no doubt a good fire had been built up for the last lap! The boiler would have been 'blowing up', the injector used to try to keep her quiet, and in due course they got the road and the driver gave her the works.

However, No 8577 slipped badly on the junction, 'caught the water' and struggled up the 1 in 58. But the roaring steam and water so evident in the photograph brought her to a stand right by the photographer. After a few minutes it was agreed that they should drop backwards down to the junction to have another go. This time they just made it, no slipping and no priming, and were on their way to Aldeburgh.

EARLY DAYS
1924–
1940.
01

My parents left Leatherhead in the late autumn of 1933 and spent the following few months in the Blue Court Hotel at King's Langley. Before long I found my way on my bicycle to the station where the work of Stanier was unheard of and the London and North Western was very much to the fore. I spent many hours on the platform in that holiday and my memory still does its job, unconsciously – for I never took notes. One day stood out above all others when a Claughton came to a stand at the down slow platform and the engine was the famous Patriot, the Memorial engine to those LNWR employees who lost their life in the 1914–18 war. I can see it all happening as if it was yesterday. The Claughton was a magnificent engine and like the GC 4 cylinder engines, had been criticised mercilessly for various defects. The GC engines if driven intelligently were very fine performers as I know from my own experience and no doubt the Claughtons were the same.

One day in February or March 1934, my parents took me with them to Amersham & Chesham Bois to look at a house. We'd travelled by bus to Rickmansworth and hence forward to Amersham by train. It was a beginning, although I did not know it, of my life as a railwayman. I remember waiting at Rickmansworth for our train which was going to Aylesbury and it came in hauled by an electric locomotive, a strange 'Bo-Bo' painted dark red and carrying a name; and as I watched, a railwayman slid down under the buffers between the engine and the Dreadnought carriage and uncoupled it from the train and in a flash he was up and giving the right-away to the driver who moved off briskly and stopped opposite a steam locomotive standing in the downside yard.

A gentle blast on the whistle and the Metropolitan tank engine dropped down onto its train and was hooked up by the same strong and fit shunter and there was just time for me to hop back in the train with my somewhat agitated parents before we left for Amersham and began to claw up the long grade largely at 1 in 105. I was fascinated, and not long after my parents, having moved home, packed me off out of the way to the station to watch the trains! From that day on I was a Great Central man and when interviewed by Mr Edward Thompson in 1940, when I had applied for a premium apprenticeship, I said that I would very much like to be a Gorton apprentice. Mr Thompson immediately said that it was out of the question and that I would be taken on at Doncaster as soon as possible. How right he was!

One evening, probably in the summer of 1936, I was on my bicycle in Stubbs Wood. Over to the right there was an extensive beech wood through which the Chesham branch of the Metropolitan and Great Central passed. At the end of the wood, a train would come into sight on its way up the hill towards Chalfont and Latimer. However, there was a very black cloud of smoke from the railway and it was obvious that there was an engine and train which had come to a stand for some reason about a quarter of a mile from me and my bike and also my home. I was immediately interested and so instinct took me to the far end of Stubbs Wood and out into Quill Hall Lane. I went down to the point where the railway comes up and over the hill on its way to Chalfont – or as it is single line – to Chesham. I had not long to wait and what should come round the curve and under the bridge but the little but sturdy E class tank engine, No 1, not unknown to the present generation. She was certainly in a hurry and disappeared round the curve, but no time had been wasted for in about 15–20 minutes along came that rather self-important No 1 leading the cavalcade of an LNER A5 and half a dozen LNER coaches. Was the train then cancelled? We shall never know but one likes to think that it would have eventually picked up its booked working.

I have memories of Amersham back to 1934 before the 'Footballers' were built and took over most of the fast trains to Leicester, Nottingham, Sheffield and Manchester. I remember when there were no flats, no offices, and no carparks on the up side but there was a sizeable goods yard under the control of Mr Taylor, the Station Master. So, there was nothing to stop me riding my bike along a path near to the railway and one evening I heard the throaty bark of an engine which literally burst under Hyron's bridge and a little E class, maybe No 1, with her driver and fireman thrashing the living daylights out of her and manfully running to time with a heavy load of commuters. This did not often happen for the Metropolitan fleet was very well maintained but things would change rapidly with the coming of hostilities.

In November 1937 the larger Metropolitan engines were transferred to the LNER depot the other side of the tracks at Neasden and a proportion of the Met men went with them and eventually those that were left became part of British Railways although they kept to their Met duties. Various interesting changes were made by the LNER and eventually the Met H class now H2 and Nos 6415–6422, once Nos 103–110 were transferred to Colwick near Nottingham, where they were extremely unpopular! Their place at Neasden was taken by Great Central engines of which both the A5 and the L1/3 classes predominated, but now and again, the LNER began to use the K class, now class L2, on passenger trains. Now, back in the earlier 20s, the growing Metropolitan goods traffic required more powerful engines for which the new Ks were to be ideally suited. Their design was to be based on that of the SECR N class of 2-6-0 design which was greatly multiplied at Woolwich Arsenal after the war but ultimately not required. So the Met bought sufficient sets of parts to have them redesigned to meet their requirements and erected as tank engines. This was done in 1925 by W G Armstrong-Whitworth and the engines, as would be expected, did splendid work until their last one was withdrawn in 1948. On the Southern in 1927, a River class tank locomotive was involved in a fatal accident near Sevenoaks and from then on until they were rebuilt, the Rivers were barred from passenger work. But the Met Ks thrived on their freight work and as a youngster I could hear the K (by then L2) working an

TOP LEFT: This little engine was a sight for sore eyes. She was taken over by the Great Western at the time of the Grouping and when I first saw her she must have been a Newbury or Reading engine. She and her two sisters were the last of the Midland and South Western Junction Railway fleet and she came up to Savernake on a Saturday evening. She was always punctual, always in good form and smart and here she is at the west end of Savernake station which you can't see because the injector on No 1335 seems to be giving trouble. She will run round her train, hook up and pause for a while and away she will go back to Newbury. On the left is the line to and from the Low Level station and also to Marlborough, Swindon and Cheltenham.

TOP RIGHT: Here is another 'Met' tank transferred to the LNER in 1938 and there was very little cleaning at Neasden in the Great Central depot during and after the war. The remaining Met engines at the old shed were still quite smart but this photograph is of a K class rebuilt from parts made for a South Eastern and Chatham design was typical of the period. The spare parts were kept at Woolwich Arsenal and the Metropolitan K class was basically rebuilt from kits made up at Woolwich and then converted by W G Armstrong-Whitworth, along with the Chief Mechanical Engineer of the Metropolitan Railway so here you have an extremely capable 'Mogul' – a tender engine converted to a 2-6-4 Tank engine.

BOTTOM: An ex-Metropolitan H class tank engine on a hot summer day so it might well be 1939. Three coach trains certainly were a rarity or else I was not about at lunchtime or early afternoon, perhaps. The Hs were handsome engines, very tall and quick off the mark providing they did not slip. The Met men had good Welsh coal. The experienced Met fireman would fill the firebox and give the Welsh lumps a good cooking and then sit down in comfort to Aylesbury and still have a nice fire ready for the return journey!

LEFT: 'Old Popey', as he was known by Buckinghamshire railwaymen. He was of course Gerald Pope, a well-known Met driver all along the line. 'Popey' as he was to everybody bar the likes of me, where it was Mr Pope.

He stands on the gangway of his A5 No 5003 (he enjoyed the Great Central engines as much as his own despite the competition) for the H class had all gone away in the early or late 40s; even this photograph which was taken in 1944–45 at Aylesbury, taking water for the journey back to Rickmansworth. He wears his Met uniform and cap (more like a chauffeur's cap of the 1920s) as did the Met men; they wanted to keep their own uniform and not change to the LNER! His overalls were like that of the Great Western and Southern. All very well, but you had to buy an extra set of braces whereas with the normal overall it was the bib and brace pattern.

In his two books on his railway life, Bill Harvey, when he was acting as Shed Master at Neasden, did some trials with the G class tanks which pleased him no end. Not only did 'Popey' follow his instructions to the letter and, in addition, overcame the steaming difficulties but he was also enjoyable company and delighted to have his shed master with him. That too would have pleased my old friend.

late evening freight train bound for Finchley Road come thumping up through the woods and cuttings to reach the summit before Amersham station. Legend had it certainly on the Southern that such an engine was unsafe but I wonder. Both young and inexperienced, I travelled on an L2 and our Driver Len Hyde and his fireman were highly delighted with the way she handled a passenger train and so was I. What's more I'm still here!

It must have been in the summer of 1947 when I was working at Liverpool Street and still living with my mother in Chesham Bois. I used to catch the 6.40am from Amersham through to Liverpool St on the Metropolitan en route to Stratford and I never remember a Met train being late and this applied to both forms of traction. I often used to ride in the front brake van on the way home as the train was very full, and I liked to be near the engine whether it was electric or steam. The Met electric locomotives used to sway from side to side and you could see this through the front window of the brake van. Furthermore you could see the driver sitting on the edge of his stool and as the train passed through Neasden and hit that old crossing, the motorman (as he was officially called) appeared to be in danger of being thrown across his cab. But he never was and he would be stopping at Harrow-on-the-Hill, then Moor Park before Rickmansworth where the steam locomotive came onto the train. The shunter had to unhook like lightning and the steam locomotive had to back on and everything had to be done in three minutes and away the steam engine would go with its six unwilling Dreadnought coaches.

The usual engine in 1947 was a Great Central A5, but on the Chesham trains it was the practice to use the C13 engine that now was working the branch, and then change over with the other branch engine for the latter to go to Neasden for servicing. That meant that there was a less powerful engine at the head and a greater likelihood of running into trouble over the severe gradients. It so happened that I had decided to travel with Len Hyde on this particular train one evening and when he coupled on at Rickmansworth, he told me quietly that his fireman was a very young hand so I offered my services, being used to both the road and the situation. The boy had got a good fire ready and full steam pressure and having pushed the fire forward and given it a good stir-up we got off to a reasonably brisk start. The safety valves began to lift and I had to put the injector on at once to maintain the boiler. The engine was a little old N5 built in the late 1890s and although they had many good points, there was no doubt that we were overloaded. I was firing either four or six shovelsful for each round and was slowly losing ground on the level of water in the boiler. Anyhow we got to Chorleywood on time and set off as soon as the guard gave us the tip. We had regained the level of the water to about half a glass with full steam pressure and as we climbed up through the woods we were reasonably optimistic that we could get through to Chalfont and beyond without stopping for a blow-up.

Away we went on time from Chalfont, but were we going to reach the summit of the Chesham branch without stopping? We carried on exactly as before, Len very much on top of the job and working the engine as economically as possible. The water was right down and just showing in the gauge glass with the regulator wide open but we were bunker-first and we reached the longed-for change of gradient. Len winked at me and we rolled down the hill to Chesham with no time lost. And both injectors working. We had made it without losing time and were mighty pleased with ourselves and the young man realised how difficult situations can be dealt with successfully. As for me I caught the next bus home to Amersham!

Len Hyde's son, always known as 'Digger' was an Assistant Motorman on the Bo-Bos at Neasden and quite by chance, I met him through missing my 11pm train home from Baker St. Believe it or not, I was still wearing overalls and clogs having come straight from work where there were no washing facilities of any description in those days in the Plant Works. I arrived at Baker St to find one of the Met Bo-Bos attached to the midnight train to Aylesbury. It was now about 1120 but still daylight enough to take a photograph and that was the beginning of a friendship with Motorman Syd Tapper and his mate, 'Digger'. What I was doing for a living came up for discussion and I was at once invited to travel in the cab all the way to Rickmansworth.

And what a world it turned out to be when we got the right-away at midnight! We struck off gently but when the controller was opened wide, there was such a cacophony of noises whilst I stood with my back a few inches from the explosions and wondered if my hour had come. It was during the black out and it was my first trip on an electrified railway. We bounced through Neasden and after Harrow, it must have been Moor Park and all stations to Aylesbury, with the change of power at Rickmansworth. Passing Northwood, Syd got up and simply said "Stop her at Moor Park!" I could not see a thing but suddenly my common sense returned and I reduced speed in plenty of time and ran in gently, which would not do in an intensive service. But there was none of the noise associated with a steam locomotive, which indicate your speed and whereabouts and which result from use and experience and, of course, of learning the road. And then there was another surprise for me. In those days, some of the Neasden motormen had the occasional weekend booked on to keep in touch with the Inner Circle. Syd would do the driving and Digger the guard's duties and they would do a round probably in both directions. Most enjoyable with the 'Guard' admonishing his motorman for losing time and hanging about.

The old inner Circle stock has long gone but it was in full use after the war when my mother was living in Kensington. If I was having a spell at Headquarters, I travelled to work and back from High St Kensington to Liverpool St, always with an Inner Circle train. Outwardly they looked the same but there was a marked difference in acceleration though I cannot remember the names of the

TOP LEFT AND RIGHT: Here is a comparison between two engines who joined forces after the formation of the SECR, although one of them was almost entirely South Eastern and Chatham design, and the other of London, Chatham and Dover design but nevertheless built for the former. No 1699 stands pre-war outside Reading shed, originally a South Eastern depot but now host to Southern engines of all sorts. And, my goodness, they were – both classes, the R1 1699 and the H class 1550 – wonderful engines. No 1550 has just been over to Victoria with empty stock and is near the top of that old 1 in 64 gradient on her way back to wherever is her next duty. I have to say that I have always felt that these engines were outstanding and they steamed so freely which is a great advantage in the South London network with its stiff gradients.

BOTTOM RIGHT: The engine is of the Great Central 'Sam Fay' class engine No 428, *City of Liverpool*, stationed at Gorton, Manchester. Don't believe all this nonsense about the 'Sam Fays' not being up to their work. This engine for several years was run by the same Driver and Fireman, Driver George Bourne and Fireman E Hailstone. Ted Hailstone I knew very well indeed and he thought the world of No 428. He taught me a great deal about railway work and often talked of working through from Manchester to London with the greatest of ease, for example on the up and down mails.

Certainly Ted admired his driver, a strict disciplinarian as was Ted himself, who also admired his Firemen such as George Howard, Maurice Saunders and Rodney Darwen who I met many years later in Liverpool. I think it is a 'visitor' in the fireman's seat and that is Ted at work filling the back end of the grate with a few down the sides and a very few to the front of the firebox. But the two Gorton men could master any situation however tough with their own engine from start to finish without a qualm. And you can see the bridge that still exists at the foot of the bank and also the beginning of the curve through the station.

contestants. Nothing strange nor was it unusual in hot weather to have the carriage doors slid wide open, well loaded and ready for the 'off' at their station. But nobody fell out, to my knowledge: they were wedged in the doorway anyhow and all the passengers knew the form just as they did on the Jazz in the steam days. The passengers on the Jazz were disciplined and the last one out had a duty to shut the doors. But we come into our own with the Jazz in 1945 as we did with things such as trials with the new B2 No 1671 against a B17 No 1638 in 1946.

Maybe Bill Collins of Neasden is so prominent in my mind because we kept in touch until he died, well into his 90s. It would be about 1904–6 when he applied to become an engine cleaner on the Great Western Railway. He was told to come back when he had grown taller. This he did and I believe he started cleaning and was in the line to be passed for firing. However, he was told that he had to stay where he was and the classic reply was "No, thank you, Sir, I'm off to join the Central" and, after he had stuffed paper in his boots to make himself up to 5ft 6" to be quite sure, he joined his brother who was already at Neasden. He was soon firing and eventually passed for driving in 1918–19 and was well on his way towards the top link when I got to know him about September 1939, just after the War started.

He and his mate, Bill Palfreyman who like many ex GC men preferred to wear a boiler suit from the Fitters and Boilermakers Club at the shed, were working the 1:50pm slow from Marylebone to Woodford which had been a Woodford job for a short time but the workings had been changed and now Neasden had it for the time being. Bill knew that I was keen to join the railway when I left school and had taken me on the front a few times so up I got. Much to my joy, the engine was No 5196, the second of the two B1s that were one of J G Robinson's early designs. No 5195 had piston-valves but ours was a flat valver: a six-wheeled coupled version of the Atlantics. Anyhow I was told to take hold and I knew what to do and knew the gradients of the road but when it came to stopping I needed guidance for it is one thing to watch and another to do! Approaching Great Missenden, he put his hand over mine to apply the brake but nothing was offered. We dropped down to Wendover and Stoke Mandeville where he took over, before we arrived at Aylesbury. What men did in those days and how keen so many of them were to share their experience with the younger end for I was barely 16. Years later, when Bill died, I went to his funeral in Marlow. The church was not far from the River Thames and the sun shone, it was a glorious day and our thoughts turned so warmly to Bill Collins, Engine Driver, and one remembered the pleasure that he had given to his mates and friends and the long service he had given to the railway.

TOP LEFT: North End Gas Works Tunnel at King's Cross in 1924. A heavy Leeds express, GC 4-cylinder B3 class No 6168. The B3 class were powerful and heavy on coal in the wrong hands but there was no option on this gradient. Future Chief Inspector Jenkins, the fireman on this engine, thought the world of her and so did his driver.

TOP RIGHT: The best of the three wonderful Copley Hill Atlantics, No 3300, still green in the Garden sidings, August 1941. Percy Hudson and Alf Cartwright were a splendid pair. Alf used to enjoy firing and was only about 54 and was a splendid driver, though Percy used to mutter that he spent more time gossiping than oiling the engine. A very droll humorist who usually wore a celluloid collar which was washed each day under the tap – as good as new next day.

BOTTOM LEFT: On the left is the Fireman John Albert Walker (Pricker Dick) ex GC from Staveley. He was a comedian and given to using the pricker due to his upbringing at Staveley near a colliery and used to working with heavy freight loads with steam being suddenly required after an hour's standing. The way to get it was to push the fire over with a pricker. Not the Copley Hill way of doing things! The Driver is John Smith ('Nookie'), quiet and sound. The engine is No 6100, class B4, in the Garden sidings at Doncaster. Albert is 'knobbing' the fire and has the big door open and building up the back end of the grate with good big lumps of Yorkshire hard coal.

BOTTOM RIGHT: Poster produced for the LNER announcing the increase of signalmen's wages. The poster shows a pair of hands manually operating the signals while a train passes by in the distance. The artwork is by Austin Cooper (1890–1964), who was born in Manitoba, Canada, and studied art in Cardiff. Cooper began his career as a commercial artist in Montreal, but returned to London in 1922 where he designed posters for LNER, Indian State Railways and London Transport.

L·N·E·R
Wages of Signalmen
for 1 Year
£1,831,647
Going·on·All·the·Time

THE FLYING SCOTSMAN

LUGGAGE LABELS

10 LARGE SIZE 1 1ᵈ

LEFT: GNR No 1 Patrick Stirling's masterpiece, built in 1870. Here she is in Cambridge Up Bay in 1938 on a special train of GNR coaches. She is virtually in her original condition minus alterations such as the fitting of the vacuum brake. The tender is not of Stirling design but over the years there have been tenders which could have been made available.

TOP RIGHT: Design for LNER labels by British silhouette artist Harry Lawrence Oakley who made tens of thousands of silhouettes between the 1920s and 1950s. Oakley produced portraits, books, newspaper illustrations, and stationery. He perfected the technique of speedily cutting folded paper with scissors, with no prior drawing, and found a good market for portraits. During his time as a soldier in the First World War he designed posters for the army.

RIGHT: May 1940, B3 No 6166, *Earl Haig*, at Amersham. This was the 8:15am Marylebone–Leicester all stations, which returned with the corresponding slow due into Marylebone at 6:06pm. The engine then worked the night mail to Leicester in both directions until the Pacifics and V2s were established. Fireman Ted Mahon, and Driver Ted Simpson, the senior driver at Neasden who hailed from Brunswick, Liverpool and came to Neasden in 1898–99 as a fireman. He had been driving since 1911 and firing on the main line for at least five years. He started on the MS&L (CLC) in 1891. He was a dear friend to me and a great encouragement in my career: he retired in April 1941, three months after I started at Doncaster.

"THE CORONATION"
ON THE EAST COAST ENTERING SCOTLAND
ITS QUICKER BY RAIL
FULL INFORMATION FROM ANY L N E R OFFICE OR AGENCY

TOP LEFT: A steamraiser lights the fire in the cab of a LMS engine in 1936, some four hours before the engine leaves the shed.

LEFT: *The Coronation* on the East Coast Entering Scotland. Poster produced in 1938 for the LNER promoting rail travel to Scotland, showing the *Coronation* locomotive travelling at speed along the coast north of Berwick, with the Longstone Lighthouse, Farne Islands Priory, Dunstanborough, Bamburgh and Holy Island Castles shown in the distance. Artwork is by Frank Henry Mason, who was educated at HMS *Conway* and spent time at sea. He painted marine and coastal subjects and was involved in engineering and shipbuilding. He designed railway posters for the NER, GWR and LNER.

ABOVE: This Class V2 2-6-2 steam locomotive No 4771 was designed by Sir Nigel Gresley (1876–1941) for the LNER and was built at Doncaster in 1936.

ABOVE: At Grantham Loco in 1941. Basil de Iongh (on the left) and myself were very young and it must have been September 1941 but it did not stop us posing on old No 4040, one of the few J4s left running and really a Newark engine. She was built in 1896 in Ivatt's time by Dübs of Glasgow but has a genuine Stirling curved topped cab with an extension bolted on in later years. She lasted until 1949 and was never reboilered to class J3.

Our Doncaster V2 had run hot and had to be replaced at Newark. Our driver was the hot-tempered Harry Moyer and we were given an 'A' engine (class J6) assisted by No 4041. As No 4041 was the leading engine, the driver correctly created the brake but for some reason Harry was upset by the Newark man's assumption. Harry went forward and as the Newark driver was not prepared to be got at by some upstart from Doncaster, there was an almighty row. The guard blew until he was purple in the face, station staff shouted and in the end the fireman on No 4041 blew the whistle and off we went.

BELOW AND RIGHT: These photos were taken during the summer of 1939. I was very friendly with an Andover (M&SWJ) driver, Arthur Wilkins, who was exceptionally kind to me as were Mr White and other signalmen at Savernake Low Level. I was at school at Marlborough and our very enlightened housemaster encouraged us to form a cricket team to play against the villages round about.

My favourite fixture was against Burbage whose team contained a fast bowler whose name was K Fear. Mr Fear was, I think, a relief porter/signalman at Savernake and the Burbage captain was Mr Bragg who, I understood, was the local ganger as well as the wicket-keeper. He was the true village cricketer who had one stupendous stroke, came in wearing a cloth cap with one pad and wearing his ordinary trousers held up with braces. No doubt he was a good railwayman too.

So we have No 3278 *Trefusis*, a Duke rather of the old school and I have to say by no means popular. Now there was a Cheltenham–Andover service which left Lansdown at 1:35pm, Marlborough 3:21pm and the seemingly deserted Savernake High Level at 3:31pm and here she is hauled by a Bulldog (right), which I think was No 3421 leaving the High Level en route to Andover. I met Arthur Wilkins again in 1943 when I came down from Doncaster, leaving about 0420 and reaching Andover in time for lunch with him and his wife and home in the early hours. And at Stewarts Lane where I also worked, we had Joe Burton who came from Andover and had fired many times for my old friend: it's a small world!

PREVIOUS PAGES LEFT: Before the war, Parkeston shed had a couple of GN Ivatt C12s: No 4016 is one of the original 1897 breed leaving Parkeston Quay for Manningtree with some old GER six-wheeled coaches. The engine was not very powerful but could stand a belting. With a full regulator, short cut-off, they tended to bounce up and down at speed!

PREVIOUS PAGES RIGHT: August 1941. Newfound friends, all ex GC men and posing for a 17-year-old boy and, although they did not know it, for posterity. From left: Fireman Percy Carline, who fired for Driver Blanchard and retired shortly afterwards; Jack Burgon, who fired for Polly Hadman and who retired at the same time; and Bob Foster, who had started about 1897, Queen Victoria's Jubilee Year. Percy and Jack had started in 1919 so had 22 years' firing when the photograph was taken. Jack, who was very knowledgeable technically, was killed in 1956 when a defect developed on his engine and he leaned out either to see or listen and hit his head on a bridge near Newark. As for Bob, he gave me great experience both in driving and firing, and remained a good friend until he was involved in an accident near Doncaster, which ended his career as a driver.

TOP LEFT: A station luggage handler surrounded by Christmas parcels and suitcases in 1936.

LEFT: A LM&S lorry delivering oil and lubricants to a garage in Northampton in 1935. These lorries collected goods to be transported by rail, and delivered goods from depots to their destination. At this time motor vehicles were starting to take over from horse-drawn transport.

ABOVE: M Type container on a lorry at St Pancras goods yard, 1933. These containers were made from steel and lined with wood, with a door at either end. They were ventilated with slats and were used for the transportation of meat. Containers had always been used by the railways. By the 1920s they were being used to transport goods from door to door without the items having to be unpacked.

RIGHT: The C5 Compound Atlantic, No 5364 *Lady Farringdon*. I have worked on her on the Cleethorpes–Doncaster line. She was excellent locomotive but long past her best. Leicester had all four in the 1920s and they ran expresses to London which were economical and fast. The Parker D5 on the left is on a Cleethorpes–New Holland service. Take note of the reducing valve on the smokebox.

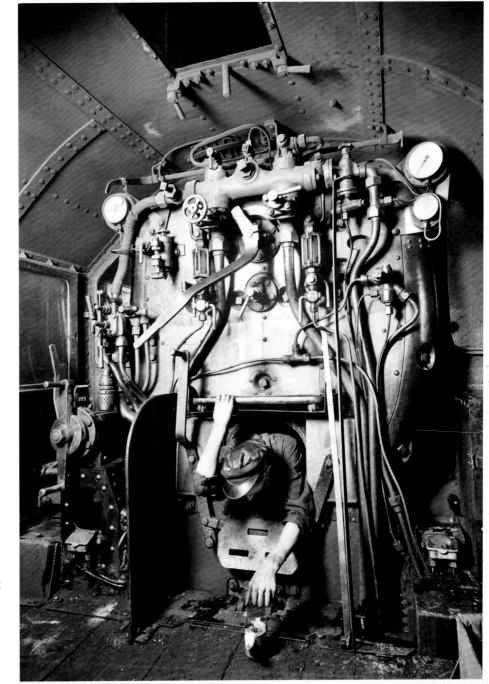

LEFT: No 7785 is an F5 'Gobbler', powerful and economical. She is making light work of a load of eight coaches up Bethnal Green bank which was 1 in 70 and will find more climbing later on in the journey. In 1945, the Enfield services were worked by similar F6s and N7s at Epping. The all-important Westinghouse pump is in full view.

RIGHT: A boilermaker after carrying out maintenance work inside a firebox, 1936.

02

WARTIME
1939–1945
DONCASTER WORKS AND RUNNING SHEDS

The Doncaster Works B and D shops were interesting and friendly but a mere prelude to my work in the Crimpsall, a tough but happy 11 months turning out repaired locomotives at a speed unthinkable before the war: but then comes the running sheds, 'Carr Loco' and that was the life for me. It took two years before I reached the Crimpsall repair shop for the first time in 1941. Working in the the machine bay with Harry Oldham was a repetitive but enjoyable job of setting return cranks on wheel sets for engines with Walchaerts valve gear. Harry was a good mate in every way and put up with my inexperience most of the time. Then after a short spell in the Millwrights, fate took me 'down t'Crimmy' again to work on Bill Umpleby's pit in 2 Bay. I was put with Edgar Joe Elvidge with whom I worked for 11 months instead of the allotted six, a great experience as we got on so well together that I asked to forego my five months in 4 Bay on the Pacifics. I had been told by a family friend that I would hear industrial language that I should never try to imitate and I got my fill from Edgar those 11 months. He called me everything, and the more he swore the more I laughed, which suited him fine. As to our work, we were at it flat out as there was a war on and the railways were doing the impossible month after month. Furthermore Edgar had a simple philosophy: he worked for the War Effort, he worked for the LNER and he worked to make as much money as he could, which didn't amount to very much. All of us liked and respected our chargehand, but Edgar used to grumble that 'Beef' Taylor's gang opposite made more money than we did, because Beef was 'good with a pencil', whereas our chargehand was not. Timekeeping was very strict and everybody clocked on next to the Machine Bay office guarded by a Wild West moustachioed gentleman wearing a Stetson who, at two minutes past the hour, would slam the cupboard door with ghoulish pleasure so that you were booked late and lost a quarter. It only happened to me once, and I grabbed my card and nearly lost my fingers instead. I worked with Edgar for nothing and then booked on after a 'quarter'.

Edgar was like many of the plant's craftsmen who had no wish to know the top brass. I doubt if he knew what H N Gresley looked like nor cared: at a pinch, he might recognise the Works Manager, F H Eggleshaw. But he was hot stuff on each Crimpsall foreman's character, although he wanted nothing to do with 'authority'. We had several erectors on our gang, all first class, and I was able to get the camera out at work now and again when we went to finish off our engine at the Weigh House. Our foreman was a Mr Andrews, who I liked as much as it is possible to do so in such disciplined circumstances, but when I was Divisional Manager in Liverpool about 1971, who should turn up out of the blue but Mr Andrews in retirement, and so we went out together for a splendid lunch at the Adelphi, courtesy of BR. He reminded me of a little incident when I was on the carpet in the office of the Superintendent of the Crimpsall. Shall I ever forget! I wanted to be first out of the gate on my bike at lunchtime and the way to do this was to get into the bike shed and then take the bike to a strategic position out of sight. Unfortunately this had been going on with others for some time and a very senior and terrifying foreman, Mr Whittaker, caught me red handed and gave me one hell of a dressing down. But that was not the end, for during the afternoon I was sent for by Mr Hawkes in his office together with Mr Andrews and Mr Whittaker. I was given a thorough telling-off by Mr Hawkes and told that the matter would be noted on my record, but I felt worse over my foreman's quiet comment: "Dick, you've let me down badly." George Andrews also told me there was nothing entered on my record card for the simple reason that I didn't have one. But it has lived with me all my life and it makes me think now when I remember how many folk I had to discipline as a shedmaster and the sort of tales that I was told until people realised that I had been through the mill too.

One thing Edgar loathed was to be sent down to the Carr Loco when one of our engines was in minor trouble after being released to traffic. There was no piecework rate attached to such work and Edgar had no room for running shed fitters, who he regarded as a crowd of ignorant bodgers. On the other hand, I was in my element and I knew that come January 1944, I should be transferred to the shed. Edgar could not understand this and told me I must be mad. But on politics, which I never discussed with him or anybody else, Edgar was firmly to the Left, whereas an old friend of his, who patched cylinders with great skill, was very well spoken and never swore, as well as being a staunch Conservative. This Mr Day deliberately talked down to Edgar, whose temper on politics was within very easy reach, and then he would say: "Now Edgar, there's no call to speak to me in those terms", his preciseness infuriating Edgar even more. Still, they were the best of friends!

This was my education in the 'University of Life', as were my studies for the ONC and HNC in Mechanical Engineering at Doncaster Tech where I showed up poorly against my friends who had left school at 14. John Stephenson and Wally West saw me through Pure Maths and I saw them through English Essay: they both got first class passes and I was lucky to get a second. Just possible I did not work hard enough.

The running shed life at the Carr was what I really wanted: the comradeship of the artisans and staff, none of whom were on the piecework that drove the Plant men relentlessly onward. Live engines, smoke and steam, excitement, the constant battle with the demands of the timetable, 24 hours a day, seven days a week, breakdowns, derailments, heat and bitter cold, football played in clogs in the lunch hour – or cricket – sometimes extended so that the foreman came after us, rough conditions, no messrooms, no changing rooms, no washing facilities except in a bucket of paraffin, yet this was the life I loved and nothing disillusioned me. Once again, although I was older by now, the men, boys and

TOP: A1 No 4477 *Gay Crusader* has had a hard war at King's Cross and is ready for a general repair. Soon in the stripping shop, then into 4 Bay Crimpsall, re-assembled with usual skill and speed, given a dab of paint, sent out for her trial, and away down south back into the rough and tumble.

BOTTOM LEFT: A Sunday morning in the summer of 1944 about 1:30pm. We had been on a lifting job that did not require a full gang and for which I would not be paid. From left: our regular guard, Fred Hague, the crane driver, Ernie Newby, George Gant, the van man who, apart from working hard, looked after the cooking, in this case breakfast, probably bully beef, bread and marge and pickles – marvellous. Remember, it was wartime: no eggs, no this and that, but gallons of tea with tinned milk to keep us going; then our foreman, Cyril Palmer, ready for off with his bike clips, Ted Booth, Syd Grindell and Stan Harrison, all long-serving and completely reliable members of the gang.

BOTTOM RIGHT: The Heavy Hammer Gang: Carr Loco brake blockers and adjusters alongside an American 2-8-0 USAA No 1720 which had passed through the plant before going overseas in August or September 1944. The photo was taken in the summer at the back end of the shed with Jack Liversedge and Jim Archer. How men have changed in their style of dress, particularly in Jack's case. The old cheap cloth cap was everywhere: usually greasy and comfortable but it provided little protection from knocks and blows to the head. But nobody worried about that sort of thing. Life was dangerous in a running shed but not so bad as all that if you kept a sharp lookout for movements or engines easing up in the shed with you underneath.

USE SHANKS' PONY

WALK
when you can

AND EASE THE BURDEN WHICH
WAR PUTS ON TRANSPORT

TOP LEFT: A mobile Air Raid Precautions unit formed by LMSR with coaches fully equipped for anti-gas training, toured the whole of the railway system training employees.

TOP RIGHT: Doncaster Plant Works, March 1943. Left: 'Stan', a Polish aristocrat who later joined the RAF where I heard that he had been killed. He was a most enjoyable character and revelled in the rough and tumble of Yorkshire industrial life. Right: my old mate Edgar Joe Elvidge, who was an Erector on Bill Umpleby's pit in the Crimpsall. He was a hard worker and I had to do my whack. I took a few pictures of him but normally there was no time for that sort of thing!

BOTTOM LEFT: Everyone was encouraged to walk during wartime whenever they could and the government issued posters to that effect.

BOTTOM RIGHT: The Weigh House staff and hangers-on against a new K3 in October 1943. Amongst those on the gangway are Pete Wright and Harold Thomas, Apprentices, with Roly Williamson, one day to be Mayor of Doncaster. Standing left-to-right: Fitters Paddy Ledger, Fred Gregson, 'Flan', Drivers Fred Elmes and Harry Capp, Chargehand Arthur Reisbeck, Driver Arthur Laver, Shunter Dick Ball, our Labourer and Steam-Raiser Dick Jackson and Examiner Cyril Wood – not much missed his eagle eye.

Each driver had two weeks on trial trips and one week on No 3980, the Crimpsall shunter: the firemen came and went on seniority, all young men by the standards of the day, but the drivers were nominated volunteers and were out of the line of promotion until they wished to return, which was a rarity – a good arrangement as all three men were vastly experienced.

lady fitter's mates were always friendly. In the Plant, most craftsmen had an apprentice learning his trade whereas at the shed, each fitter had a mate who was not a craftsman but came to know a great deal of the fitter's work and what was needed in an emergency. There were about 12 craft apprentices at the Carr and after seven years of hard training, they had the makings of becoming first class running shed fitters, with a very wide knowledge of the faults and weaknesses of a large variety of steam locomotives. In the war their work became increasingly difficult especially at a depot with a great deal of freight work such as Mexborough or, indeed, Doncaster.

In late October 1944, soon after my birthday, I was told that my time was up at the Carr Loco and that next week I should report at 9:00am in the Locomotive Drawing Office where plans for the great engines of the past and present and future had been drawn up. I was very sorry to leave my friends of nearly a year and I had learned a fair amount about life in a running shed, about relations between management and staff and about things in general but, for all that, I was very raw but very happy for not everybody had had such a fruitful and happy existence and I think that that was the last time that I went into the Carr. Over the years I got once to an enquiry window and that was about all from that day to this!

I was sent for by Mr Oakes, who was the District Locomotive Superintendent, and had a very helpful if short interview with him; but he gave me a lot of food for thought which convinced me all the more that I wanted to be a running man for the foreseeable future. He was dead right and I never looked back (maybe once) until the end of this departmental style of management. Both Charlie Walker and Cyril Palmer, the two Mechanical Foremen, sent for me and in later years, I saw Cyril rise up the ladder until he became Motive Power Officer for the GN Line. His views on Doncaster and other Drawing Offices back in 1945 were illuminating but 'Pop' Hinchcliffe at the desk behind me had regarded us Loco men with scorn and his views of the Carr were unprintable – all good fun and must not be taken to heart although I was too young and junior to answer back in those days. When dealing with a superior you did no such thing!

But now to the Drawing Office. I was placed at a vacant drawing board between two very experienced men, 'Pop' Hinchcliffe and the very tall Kenneth Kingsley. 'Pop' let it be known at once that he did not approve of steam locomotives – filthy, dirty things completely out of date. He believed in electrification and had had a great deal to do with the development of the splendid electric locomotive No 6701 now resting from whatever labours came its way in the Doncaster Works Paint Shop. The line that she might well have worked was the Great Central out of London Road to Sheffield and Wath by which time 'Pop' would probably have retired, a pity for he knew his stuff. Mr Windle never spoke to me although Mr Gray, his Geordie number two, did make the occasional dour remark as he passed my board. Over the few months that I was in the drawing office there, I was allowed to design several small items including the lubricator drive on the rebuilt 4470 whereupon I was told gleefully by Pop that "The sooner, Hardy, you get back to those dirty old steam engines, the better!" In fact, I had had great difficulty at first in sleeping so I took an evening trip down to Grantham on the 5:30pm Leeds–King's Cross the next evening. And bless me, it was No 10000 that rolled in with Grantham men and she kept me busy with that big firebox and so did No 4475, coming back with Walter Ayres on the stroke of retirement and George King who I met many years later when I was Divisional Manager at King's Cross and when he was in his 60! Remarkable really how one rarely forgot a face and a friendship.

There were some splendid engineers amongst the draughtsmen at Doncaster. Barney Symes, a small and vigorous man who was very friendly with my Chief to be, Terry Miller, at Stratford and who did a great deal for me personally and let me say that Terry finished his career as Chief Mechanical and Electrical Engineer of British Railways. The HSTs were his work. He was responsible for their design and performance but he had scant reward for his labours other than those close to him. There was Ted Parker who was responsible for the design of the B1 and there again, you rarely hear him mentioned.

It was a strange life but I made some good friends, none more so than Betty Stratford-Tuke whose husband, Athol, was serving as Group Captain RAF. Her mother was a sister of Edward Thompson and they lived in a house right at the end of Balby where the 'Trackless' turned round. I visited them on a Sunday evening from time to time and met Betty's son Robin, a few years younger than me. And then, soon after, in June 1945, I was sent for by ET, a day that I shall never forget, who told me he "was sending me to Mr Leslie Parker at Shenfield" for interview. He also wished me good luck and that might have been the end of the story. ET retired a year later after a very difficult time during and after the War: he wrote to me from time to time, very friendly and encouraging letters and then he died in 1954. Betty had moved away from Doncaster to the Kent coast where my wife and I went to see her and that was that until about three years ago when Barry Hoper of Transport Treasury received a letter from a Mrs Parfitt wishing to buy copies of the photo that I took in 1945 in Doncaster of Betty, her son Robin and Margaret, ET's sister. Barry said that this would interest me and through that old photograph of mine, we linked up again for Robin was still around with Wendy, his wife living in Sherborne and Amanda who wrote to me from Gillingham and 'Uncle Ned' is well remembered from way back. And my lovely blue-inked Parker 51 fountain pen was a gift from Robin Stratford-Tuke when he could no longer write. Some treasure! What memories!

TOP: LNER workers being served tea in the wagon workshops at Temple Mills in July 1941.

BOTTOM LEFT: Our lady labourer, Phoebe Cliff, stands with some of Bill Umpleby's men beside an old 'W' class D2 No 4398 and shedded in 'foreign' territory at Botanic Gardens, Hull. We had just turned her off our pit, tarred and feathered, as most of the painting was done while we were working on the engines in the Crimpsall 2 Bay. No 4398 would have been on our pit for six maybe seven days, and away into traffic without a trial trip. The Carr Loco would run her in on some tiddlybunk job and off she would go off to Hull. The K2s, K3s and C1 Atlantics took a few days longer and the little engines paid us best on piecework, J3/4, J6, C12, J52, N1 and N2 and such like. Not all the gang is present. From left: Wally Sysman, son of a well-known Doncaster driver; George Sparrow; 'Pat', who had just joined from outside the industry; Edgar; Phoebe, who kept us in order with her sharpish tongue; and George Holmes. It was nearly 70 years ago and it seems like yesterday.

BOTTOM RIGHT: Poster produced for the entire railway system to publicise the war effort. The passenger train on the left is giving way to the one on the right which is loaded with cannons. From June 1940 East Coast shipping was heavily cut back and much of this freight was transferred to rail. On some sections, traffic rose by 500 per cent.

All Clear for the Guns
ON
BRITISH RAILWAYS

ABOVE LEFT: Poster produced for Southern Railways in 1945 announcing the imminent re-decoration of 800 SR stations, which would be undertaken once workers and materials were obtained. The image shows three outstretched hands holding paintbrushes, painting arcs of green and yellow paint. Artwork by L A Webb.

ABOVE: Lincoln Cathedral and 'Uphill' in the distance. We are 'Downhill' at Lincoln Loco where we are lifting in a new turntable for the Outdoor Machinery Department with the Doncaster Cowans Shildon 45-ton crane. It was a nice job on a warm day in 1944. It was also memorable in that Syd Grindell, Fitter's Mate, dropped the end of a sleeper on the toe of one of my clogs. More through shock rather than pain, it drew the F-word from me at the top of my voice which convulsed the entire gang and foreman Cyril Palmer with laughter in which I soon joined. With clogs, I didn't even lose a toe nail!

The poster text reads:

SHABBY?

Yes! This station does need smartening up. It will take time to see to over 800 S.R. stations. but it will be done as soon as we get the men and materials.

SOUTHERN RAILWAY

Keep 'em moving

EVERY WAGON IS NEEDED
There are only 4 to do the work of 5

WE MUST SPEED LOADING AND UNLOADING

It's useless making more goods if we can't move them

A DAY SAVED ON 'TURNROUND' IS WORTH 100,000 WAGONS

QUICKER 'TURNROUND'

—helps Britain deliver the goods

ABOVE: The engine is an N2 No 4722. Why we selected it, I would not know, but to three of us, an engine was an engine. From right: John Hyde, Denis Branton, 'Audrey' and myself. When I started at the Plant in January 1941, I was sent to learn a turret lathe in B Shop with Denis on days and John on afternoons. By coincidence, the three of us were also in Bill Umpleby's gang in 2 Bay in 1943. I never met anybody less like an 'Audrey', but I suppose it might have been his surname used as a mark of affection. All were craft apprentices serving seven years to become journeymen. Denis finished as one of the chargehands in the New Erecting Shop and John retired as Production Manager at York Works, for many a craft apprentice rose up from the ranks. As for me, I had grown from a skinny nipper at 17 to a fairly muscular boy. Back, arms, chest and strong hands were developed by hard work and heavy lifting. Try me for a handshake!

ABOVE RIGHT: Poster produced for the Ministry of Transport during the war to remind railway workers that due to a shortage of wagons, they must speed up loading and unloading in order to keep all the wagons moving. Artwork by Folkard-Robert.

LEFT: At the Carr Loco running shed: Flo, Reenie and Dorothy were all Lightwork Fitter's Mates and were all welcome, which says a lot for them in a man's world. They are with Herbert Ealham, an outstanding man and Fitter's Mate and his Regular Fitter, Gilbert Holden, a most friendly man. In those days it was unheard of for even the hardest swearing man to do so in front of ladies. On one occasion I was in a smokebox letting drive at some steam pipe nuts with a big hammer while my mate held the long chisel bar (we had to split the nuts). I misfired and hit my mate instead. He let drive at me but with the corner of his eye he saw a girl clerk from the office passing our engine. He jumped down and went after the girl to apologise. When he returned he carried on with me where he had left off!

ABOVE: With men called up, women entered the workforce on an unprecedented scale to replace them. In these images promoting work on the railways, so essential for the war effort, Mrs Molly Temperley does signal maintenance work, a lady train guard begins work at Victoria station in July 1943, and a woman railway worker cleans the tubes of a locomotive at London locomotive depot in about 1941 – one of a series of drawings and paintings of the St Pancras Locomotive Cleaning and Goods Yard created by Cliff Rowe.

LEFT: About once every three months when work permitted it Edgar said I could go on a trial run if anybody was daft enough to take me. But the trial crews always welcomed a visitor and here we are with the K3 No 159 which we had turned off our pit the previous day. In the picture is Fireman Roly Williamson and Driver Fred Elmes, quiet, calm and experienced. There were three Trial Drivers: Fred, Harry Capp and Arthur Laver, all volunteers and carefully vetted for knowledge. Two were on trials and the third did the Crimpsall shunting with No 3980, the old Stirling J52. The guard appeared from one of the signal boxes on the triangle and we gave him a lift home to Claypole, bike and all!

BOTTOM: Edgar (right) minus the cap that was part of his attire, with two other gentlemen of the Crimpsall. Left is Frank Sutton, Storesman. To start the day, I called on Frank for the tallow candles, which we screwed into nuts and were our only source of lighting underneath an engine, whereas at the Carr Loco, the fitters all had acetylene lamps, which had their moments and, if sworn at, would answer with a jet of flame about a foot long. Mr Day (I always called him this) in the centre was a remarkable craftsman who patched cylinders. He was well-spoken and never used bad language and, whereas Edgar was staunch Labour, the old gentleman was as blue a Conservative as ever lived. He and Edgar were good friends and it was a joy to hear them arguing, with Mr Day lecturing from his poop deck the ever more vitriolic Edgar.

RIGHT: The old K3 is waiting to be stripped for general repair and she looks a rough old thing. From left: Harry Oldham was my Fitter in the Machine Bay; Edgar, my mate, in 2 Bay; Jimmy Jewell, Edgar's friend and Boilermaker; Ted Micklethwaite, Rivetter, who was often on our pit and making a diabolical noise next to us; and a boilermaker whose name I have forgotten. I never cease to marvel that such tough characters were so happy to be photographed for I now have a treasured social history.

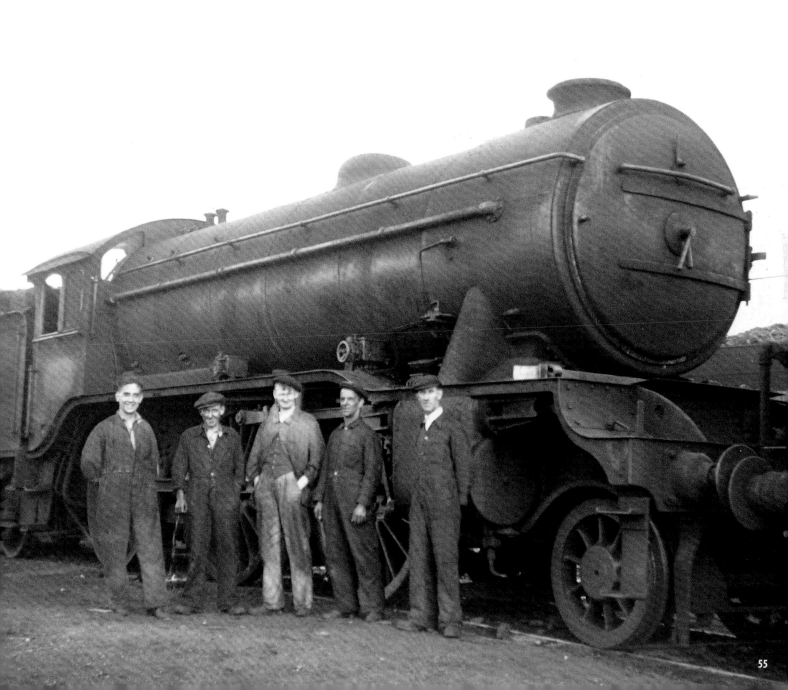

LEFT: The Yankee 2-8-0 No 1888 had come into Doncaster plant in spring 1943 for some fettling before going to work on the LNER at March. We were not employed on the work but Bill Umpleby and his gang wanted their photo taken against this engine. How different people looked in those days: we came to work on bikes, on foot or on the shiny seated 'Trackless Trams'. Bill, our Chargehand, led a happy crew, although his honesty with the pencil when calculating piecework payments used to infuriate Edgar, who was after every penny that could be earned. From left: Wally Sysman on smokeboxes; Bill Umpleby Chargehand Erector; Phoebe Cliff, our Labourer; 'Audrey', another Apprentice; Edgar Elvidge, pistons, valves, rods and motion; and Harry Waring, pipework and fittings.

ABOVE: King George VI and Queen Elizabeth at Doncaster works in 1941. The King and Queen visited the works to see the different phases of locomotive building. They met members of staff, from the managers to the workers on the factory floor and Mr Edward Thompson, the Chief Mechanical Engineer of the LNER, is on the Queen's left.

ABOVE LEFT: LNER parcel van, 21 April 1944. These vans collected parcels from stations and took them into offices and warehouses in towns; they also collected parcels to be taken to the station, providing a full door-to-door service. By this time most horse-drawn LNER vehicles had been replaced by motor transport.

ABOVE: The East Coast Main Line and its centres of engineering like York were prime targets for the German air force between 1940 and 1943. In this image, the A4 class 4-6-2 steam locomotive No 4469 *Sir Ralph Wedgwood* lies damaged in the wreckage of York North locomotive depot, following an air raid on 29 April 1942.

RIGHT: *The Mallard*, looking the worse for wear and in need of a general overhaul. From left: Peter Townend, later shedmaster at King's Cross Top Shed where he was the right man at the right time and is the acknowledged expert on Doncaster Pacifics and V2s; Bill Taylor specialised in electric traction and became a senior Electrical Engineer on the LM at Derby; Jack Taylor, who was the son of the C&W engineer and who left the Southern many years ago; Henry Steel who stayed with BR until 1949 and then served the railway in East Africa; Alan Coggan, the son of a GC driver from Keadby who, after transfer to Doncaster, found himself firing on the A1 No 4481 still with short travel valves and a rough driver who emptied the tender going to London and back. Alan has been all over since leaving the railway and now lives in Switzerland. On the gangway is David Sandiland, and I'm on the right.

ABOVE: In December 1943 the Crimpsall 'Humpy' was a departmental engine but carried its old No 3980, class J52, which had been built a month before Pat Stirling died in 1895. She was manned in turn by the trial drivers and their mates. The A4, just out of the Crimpsall, is No 4466, recently renamed *Sir Ralph Wedgwood*, as the engine that had carried the name, No 4469, was damaged beyond repair in an air raid on York in 1942, as shown on page 58. No 4466 has just been lit up for the following day's trial run.

RIGHT: VE Day celebrations in the Strand, London, 8 May 1945.

WARTIME
1939–1945
FOOTPLATE STAFF 03

The camaraderie of the footplate and the skills required were not part of my training but unofficially enginemen went to endless trouble to teach me the art of firing and then driving. During a career in which enginemen played so great a part, this experience was unforgettable.

All three of the Copley Hill GN Atlantics were world beaters and one vile evening early in 1943, Driver Bill Denman had No 4433, blowing off light at 155psi, yet he managed to start 14 coaches, packed to the roof with service personnel, a seemingly impossible task. Bill was a quiet, charming, thinking engineman who never got excited, whatever the odds. He had just come from Doncaster in 32 minutes with two stops (remember the load!) and reached Wakefield Westgate a minute early after one of those breathtaking arrivals, the speciality of the Leeds men over the 99 arch viaduct and stopping six coaches past the short down platform.

The right-away was quietly given by the Fireman, Jim Edison, Bill opened the regulator and nothing happened. No 4433 was a piston valve engine and easy to reverse with the throttle wide open. Four times he did this but she would not move forward. And then the fifth time, she inched away slowly, oh so slowly. Not a word was said but she kept moving quietly forward until, with a glorious bark from the chimney, she was on her way up the heavy grade to Ardsley. Bill had lost several minutes at Westgate so he let rip down the 1 in 100 and the old engine was rocking and rolling faster and faster but perfectly safely. Now Jim Edison had not quite recovered his nerve after a serious derailment at Bramley and when they struck Beeston Junction with a tremendous roll and headed for the over-bridge on the curve short of Beeston station (which always looked too tight a fit), he called to his mate: "Steady, Bill, for God's sake, we shall all be killed," and Bill smilingly replied: "That's alright, Jim, don't worry, I'll be with you." The following week, Harry Hornby, the archetypal GN man who had no room for ex GC men, asked Bill if what he had heard about the start at Westgate was true. Bill quietly told him what had happened and Harry shook him by the hand and said, "Well, Bill, I couldn't have done it," a remarkable complement to which Bill rarely referred but which he never forgot. But what a man!

Another time, in 1941, I was going to take an LMS friend of mine into the West Riding from Sheffield Victoria via Penistone and Barnsley so we left Sheffield at 3.30pm behind another GN Atlantic No 3296 from Lincoln. At Penistone we walked the few yards to the engine to thank the driver for a good run. He asked us who we were and where we were going and said, "Well, b....r Barnsley, you're coming with me to Manchester but one at a time." So up got Dick Lawrence and he had a good rock and roll down past Crowden after the Woodhead tunnel. Coming back, Joe Oglesby said (as he was to say more than once over the next four years), "Right, take her up the bank and don't spare my mate." Old No 3296 was a slide valve Atlantic so she pulled at my arms when notching up but I found the notch she liked to accelerate gradually up the hill and Joe relieved me before we plunged into the great tunnel. This was the first of many journeys that I made with this wonderful man and my last with his mate, Joe Antcliff, was in March 1942 and hereon lies a tale.

In 1999, I gave a talk to the Railway Club which had been advertised in *Rail News* and when I arrived, the Secretary gave me a letter. I opened it and could hardly believe my eyes. It was from J Antcliff to the secretary of the Railway Club.

'Dear Sir
On reading the *Rail News* for January I noticed that a certain Mr R Hardy is to give a talk on Railway Management. I myself am a retired Driver now in my 91st year and was stationed at the old Neepsend depot before moving to the new Depot at Darnell during the last War. What I would like to know is, is your speaker the same Richard Hardy who was an apprentice at Doncaster about the year 1941 and was always interested in the practical side of the job and would spend his weekends travelling on engines to gain experience? Two occasions I clearly remember was when I was firing for Driver J Oglesby when Richard came with us to Manchester and back through the old Woodhead tunnel and on another occasion a Saturday night trip to Leicester and back after which I think my mate took him home for a wash and brush up and breakfast before letting Richard go back home to Doncaster. Richard was a very likeable young man and a pleasure to have him around.
Yours Sincerely
J Antcliff
P.S. Hope Richard is well.'

How many old people of 90 and not given to letter writing, would take the trouble to do so after an interval of 57 years since we said goodbye that morning on Victoria station. Unbelievable, but there it was and I rang him on Sunday morning. "Here I am, Joe, it was me!" and I told him that I should be in Sheffield shortly giving a talk to the RCTS, who kindly ferried him from his home and back and so we met again after all those years. There he was, fresh-faced and smiling, far younger than 90 and we met at least twice more and had everything in common. His ambition was to go through the Channel Tunnel and it was all arranged for him to travel on the engine but he was called into hospital for a hip operation so it never came about. So yet again, what a man and the railway was full of such people.

TOP LEFT: With my great mentor Ted Hailstone at Ardsley, summer 1944. We are at Ardsley station in the slow road and we have No 4602, superheater, another splendid engine. The day we met, he said, "I've taken a liking to you, young man. If you come with me, I'll make a fireman out of you and then a driver." He was as good as his word, and for many, many thousands of miles I have practised the principles he drilled into me.

TOP RIGHT: A wartime photograph in 1943. Driver Jack Kitching, ex Barnsley and in the Piped Goods Link at Neasden, and his ex GN (New England) mate Cecil White at Princes Risborough. I would come down from Doncaster on the Aberdonian leaving at 4:20am, if on time, and travel with Jack on the 11:20am to Woodford via the New Line, all stations, even Wotton and Akeman Street, and return with the 3:05pm all stations to Marylebone via the Met. Note the blacked-out cab window, the nameplate *Jutland*, and brasses painted over at Gorton Works. Engine No 5504, class D11 shedded at Neasden. Jack came south in the early days of the GCR and Cecil was a rare GN man at a GC shed.

BOTTOM LEFT: Bob Foster and Ernest Fearnley with old No 6100, class B4, in the bay waiting for Abe Lawrence to bring the empty stock into the Western platform at Doncaster for the 5:37pm slow to Leeds. By the look of the smokebox door, she has been at Bradford on those London jobs up the 1 in 45 out of Exchange.

BOTTOM RIGHT: Staff poster produced for BR to remind staff to label train wagons clearly. The poster illustration shows a railway worker with a lamp, looking at a wagon label. Artwork by Frank Newbould (1887–1951).

HELP the shunter Use crayon or a thick black pencil and **BLOCK LETTERS** on wagon labels. Take care label is not hidden by sheet

BRITISH RAILWAYS

TOP: York, Lanky yard, with a Jubilee behind in 1945. A Sheffield C1 No 3273, with Fireman Cyril Golding and Driver Joe Oglesby of Darnall. We had come from Sheffield Victoria with the 3:20pm flyer to York via Doncaster and Selby. Cyril went in the first coach and as we ran into Rotherham, having come round the curve at a good 50mph with the station in sight, Joe said, "Over here quick and stop her at the platform." This was typical of Joe who always had some unknown challenge to keep you on your toes. That was also the day that I trapped my foot under the fall plate between engine and tender at York. In the yard known as the 'Lanky Loco', there were some sharp curves and the fall plate sprung up, my foot slipped down and I was trapped with the wood of my clogs taking the weight. Joe put the tender handbrake hard on, leaked the vacuum brake off the engine and gave her steam. She went ahead a few inches, out came my clog, the wood a bit squeezed but my foot none the worse – a lesson learned for I was standing between the uprights, one arm on the tender, one arm on the engine, rather pleased with myself and not concentrating. The photograph shows the very Spartan working conditions on the GN Atlantics, the boiler fittings can be seen and the driver and fireman were both standing, which was their normal position as the seats were virtually non existent. But the Atlantics were marvellous engines so nobody minded how badly they rocked and rolled.

BOTTOM LEFT: Bradford Exchange early in 1945. A GC N5, No 5901, a good strong little engine but with quite big cylinders. The fire had to be in perfect shape and the firing exact and the boiler not too full, otherwise there would be trouble. When I took this photo, I had left the injector at work and when I got back, I had too much water in the boiler and paid the penalty, much to Harold Binder's amusement, for I had neither 'stee-am ner watter' at our first stop, St Dunstans. But, by hard work I made it to Queensbury up the fearful bank and all was well. The group, from left: George Howard, 50 years of age and just passed for driving with his young Fireman, Hughie Cansfield. Harold Binder next to George, a GC man from Immingham and a very dear friend. He has the City of Bradford coat of arms in his cap. On the right is his regular mate, Fireman Harry Smith, 48 years of age.

BOTTOM RIGHT: Autumn 1943, Garden sidings, Doncaster, No 231 K3. It's a Sunday afternoon with my mother, a wonderful sport who had lived in Russia before and during the Revolution. In 1920 (aged 39) she married my father, who was 49 and had been a tea planter in Ceylon before the First World War. When he came home, he joined up and spent much of the war in France. Here she is, very much in wartime clothes, with Driver Bill Denman and Fireman Jim Edison, all three completely at home in each other's company.

ABOVE: In 1944 Copley Hill had more than one Pacific and here is No 2552 *Sansovino* behind the Doncaster North box. The hatchet faced Fireman, Matt Duck, had left Ernest Hine and was now in the top link, near enough 50 years of age and still firing, but not for long for by 1944 things had begun to move much more quickly, especially after the battle for Europe. He was a very good fireman and very strong, although Thernie Marsden was a light driver. I remember when No 2552 was a Neasden engine as I was about to join the railway.

RIGHT: Easter 1944 and the B1 No 8301 *Springbok* is about 16 months out of Darlington Works. We had a good run to London from Sheffield with three different crews and 11 cars, a very fair load for such a heavy road although the GC B3s often hauled up to 14 on the night trains. Driver Bill Shepley and Fireman Arthur Jepson of Gorton had brought the 9:50am from Manchester London Road and inside two minutes they had agreed not only to have their photo taken but Arthur said that he was quite happy to sit on his seat to Nottingham.

LEFT: Two railway workers pose for a photograph beside the tracks on Hest Bank Water troughs between Lancaster and Carnforth.

TOP RIGHT: March 1945 in the 'Lanky Loco' on the up side at York station. Driver Joe Oglesby of Darnall was a lovely man and the sort of mate that firemen dreamed of, and so did I. We became very great friends and I fired for him to Manchester, Leicester, York, Cleethorpes and once to Liverpool. We had worked the 3:20pm SO Sheffield – York via Rotherham (GC), Mexborough, Doncaster and Selby. Joe always had a surprise up his sleeve. I fired for him on this journey with his mate Cyril Golding in the train. We stopped at Selby after a real dash across the flat from Doncaster. Joe asked, "What have you got in there?" (meaning the firebox). "Enough for York when it's levelled with the poker." "Right, take her to Challoners Whin", and over the other side I went for the final stretch to the outskirts of York. Our engine is No 4452, a Sheffield Atlantic, the first piston valve superheated C1 built at Doncaster in 1910.

BOTTOM RIGHT: A remarkable pair. The Fireman, Percy Thorpe, is on the gangway with Benny Faux of Ardsley, as always doing the driving on a C14 en route to Ranskill Munitions Factory at Doncaster, taking water. Benny was an amazing character. He was, to some extent, a daredevil who enjoyed himself at work but never talked about it off the job. He knew exactly what he was doing but if he could shock his comrades, he would do so. He took me under his wing and taught me some of the dodges that management was not supposed to know. I was nearly always the driver when I went with him and he would leave it all to Percy and me, taking no apparent interest in what we were doing. But when he had a younger fireman, he was every button on duty and did his own job. My great mentor, Ted Hailstone, would never have dreamt of letting me see the seamy side of the job and used to grumble "I can't think what you see in that Faux!"

LMS THE DAY BEGINS

LEFT: Poster produced for the LMS in 1946 showing the locomotive *City of Hereford* undergoing early morning maintenance on a turntable surrounded by various LMS engines in the Willesden depot, London. Artwork by Terence Cuneo, son of the artists Cyrus and Nell Cuneo. He studied at the Chelsea and Slade Art Schools and in addition to a long career designing railway posters, he painted portraits and ceremonial and military subjects.

RIGHT: We had reached Aylesbury after a perfect journey with the B1 No 8301 *Springbok* and there was just time to take this photo of my friend from home, Donald Douglas, and next to him, Driver Jack Proctor, by then the Senior Driver at the Neasden, and an old friend from my boyhood days, together with Fireman Charlie Simpson, who lost his life at Barby in 1955.

BELOW: No 406, a piston valve Atlantic class C1 was turned out of Doncaster Works just before Christmas 1943, a fortnight before I left the Plant for the Carr Loco. It is in steam and will go on its trial trip next day when Dick Jackson, Weigh House labourer, has coaled it. One of the three Trial Drivers, Harry Capp, Fred Elmes or Arthur Laver would be in charge of the engine. The piston valve engines had a round piston gland, most of them had dummy tailrod guides and most, but not all, had smokebox saddles. All slide valve engines had oval piston glands and the spindle glands tended to blow, in cold weather, up the boiler side when starting. No wonder with a 32 element superheater these engines were 'world beaters'. The livery is shown to perfection. From 1941, if not before, all engines were turned out of Doncaster and other works in unlined black, and the painting was done not in the paint shop but on the engine as it was being assembled by us!

LEFT: A J52, No 4250, on the downside carriage pilot at Doncaster station in the Western bay platform, 1945. On the left is Driver Abe Lawrence, always on the late turn, and he used to view my activities with the Leeds men with a jaundiced eye until we got to know each other and he became kindness itself. Shunting was carried out carefully, no histrionics and without hurry, but always to time. Normally, the fireman (a young hand) was never allowed to drive but today he has Charlie Carter, a passed Fireman, so Abe spent the day on the other side, a pleasant change.

BELOW: A Doncaster C1 which started life as No 1421, a 4-cylinder compound built in 1907 but converted to a piston valve 2-cylinder superheated Atlantic in 1920. As a compound her Fireman for some time was George Wilson in the top link along with his brother Fred in my time at Doncaster. We are at Botanic Gardens on a Sunday afternoon with Fireman Arthur Gell and the fiery Harry Moyer, who had a brother at Grimsby, a GC man and some years older than Harry, who was in the Atlantic link. Harry got on well with Arthur, who was in a lower link and who had changed over with Harry's regular mate with whom he did not get on too well for Harry was not by any means sunshine and light with his mates if they did not measure up. He was a very good engineman and a perfectionist and nothing wrong with that.

LEFT: Probably the only photograph taken at the Thorp Arch factory, which was an enormous wartime munitions works. It was taken in June 1945, in the sidings where the trains were stabled between arrival and departure. We brought the incoming shift on duty and went round the factory railway with its four stations. We stabled the train, turned on the angle, and coupled up once more to our train to go tender first round the factory picking up the shift going home; run round once more and right away home. On Saturday and Sunday nights, we had the railway to ourselves and could get home as quick as it was safe to do.

This is a Sunday afternoon and we have the best of the very good bunch of B4s, No 6101, a real clipper. On the left, we have a factory policeman. While we were at war, the factory police were everywhere watching to see we did not move away from our engine. Then we have our guard, with a trilby hat. He was a lovely man, endlessly helpful, who was normally a Westgate passenger shunter, and he earned his living alright. Then, in the centre, is Alistair Kerr who was Deputy Land Agent at the County Hall in Wakefield, a vastly knowledgeable student of railway affairs who knew Benny Faux well and later married his daughter, Elsie. Leaning on the buffer with his cap over his nose is Benny himself, then his Fireman for the day, Fred Wilson, and finally the Thorp Arch Yard Foreman, Mr Cattermole, whose son was a Darlington premium apprentice some years younger than me.

RIGHT: The old Bradford C12, No 4524, spent much of her time working between Bradford, Halifax and Keithley. Driver George Hutchinson was a pleasant man but camera shy – the only West Riding engineman I met who did not want his photo taken. We have taken on water at Keithley in the GN platforms and the Fireman, Stan Pilsworth, poses with pleasure. No 4524 clawed her way very well up the bank to Ingrow, which we believed to be a much heavier road than the Midland Worth Valley branch that had a poor old Midland tank engine, not given, in our opinion, to heavy work. We thought nothing of the Midland and the Lanky was just bearable!

TOP LEFT: A Sunday, 2:00pm, early 1944. Garden Sidings, Doncaster: Fred Holdsworth and myself, now growing out of my overalls. K3 231 is waiting to go up to the station and to take over a typical huge wartime train of 18–19 coaches that had left King's Cross some four hours before. Fred had been a long time in the Goods Link at Copley Hill but had moved up into No 2 Tanky Gang and his mate who took the photograph was my friend Stan Hodgson who had done so much back in 1941 to introduce me to the West Riding. Stan actually came to my retirement party in 1982: what a gathering that was and how Gwenda and the family enjoyed themselves. Fred was an old GC man from Wakefield shed when it closed in 1924 and he loved his clogs. He was a very good engineman which pleased Stan who expected Fred, as a Poggy man (nickname for men who worked on the Great Central), to be heavy handed. As for me, I had to scrounge overalls and cap, and I was never short, but either I had grown or they had shrunk!

BOTTOM LEFT: A Sunday afternoon in 1944 behind the North signalbox. A Doncaster V2 in place of a K3, with Johnny Jeffs (right) and Syd Watson. Johnny was Chairman of the LDC, I think: a very good engineman and very kind to me but hot-tempered so I was told, but I had no experience of LDCs in those days. I was to find that the fiery man was often a 100 per center and both Johnny and his colleague, Ernest Clarke, were straight and to the point. Syd was also splendid value. In 2010 Barry Hoper had an email from a lady in Brisbane who was tracing her family tree. Some of her family lived in Leeds by the name of Jeffs and I had taken a photograph of Driver Johnny Jeffs in 1944–5 which is on the Transport Treasury website. We sent her the picture and some others and in the end I was linked up to Tom Jeffs (Johnny's son) and his son John, and was able to link them up with Barbara Tuck in Australia. When I first traced Tom on the phone we spent 45 minutes talking about Copley Hill men, which gave us both the greatest pleasure. He was going to be 90 in four days time and Barry had some of the Copley Hill photos printed for him and to arrive on his birthday. What could be better?

LEFT: The late summer of 1942 not long before Jack Burgon went up to pass for driving early in 1943. A splendid portrait of both men: Jack Burgon, the great enthusiast despite his 23 years of firing and Arthur Moss with his arthritis so bad that it was a struggle to get up and down from the cab, and yet he did his work without complaint. No doubt, Jack did the oiling and examination for him. Arthur was inclined to be heavy with an engine and did not run downhill very fast but they got on remarkably well. Arthur has a nice pair of clogs. The engine was one of the Doncaster new V2s in the 365 series, built at Darlington in 1942. Why Copley Hill had her on what was normally a K3 turn, I cannot remember. The set on the right is old NER stock, probably a Hull set. Botanic men came into the Garden sidings about 8:30pm and stood alongside us. The V2 would work the 10:01pm ex London back to Leeds on the double summer time.

LEFT: Here are the Eastern Headquarters Inspectors sometime in 1948 and apart from me standing in front of the smokebox, we are the Eastern leg of the HQ team plus the Chief Inspector Sam Jenkins. So standing at the back are Bill Morris, the oil Inspector who had been a driver and fireman, Tommy Sands, who was an M&GN man and standing is Len Theobald, an old friend who had been Chief Inspector GE section. Then Sam Jenkins, well known from his exploits at King's Cross, especially his guidance where necessary on the famous run of *Mallard* in 1938. Next to him is Horace Emery, the Examining Inspector for the Eastern Region and finally our Clerk, Harold Bonnett, who came from Grantham.

BOTTOM: Derek King, with Fireman Albert Walker and Driver John Smith beside the famous war memorial engine, No 6165 *Valour*, class B3 in the Garden Sidings and waiting for time to move up to the station. The engine has just passed through Gorton for a general overhaul and the brasswork has been painted over as a wartime measure. They are working the very heavy Colchester to Leeds train and a powerful engine is needed to start such a train at Wakefield on the 1 in 100 gradient.

RIGHT: Bethnal Green Bank. Here is a D15 'Claud' at the top of the gradient of 1 in 70. By the look of things the fireman is giving her a round of coal with the firehole door wide open. The head code tells us they are bound for Southend: and on the left is Spitalfields goods yard and on the extreme right the suburban lines which turn sharply to the left after Bethnal Green station. He has the road as can be seen by looking at the back of the signals and all is set with a reasonable load of old GE suburban stock for a comfortable journey to Southend Victoria.

EAST ANGLIA AND WOODFORD HALSE

1946–1952.

04

King's Lynn, a bitter wind off the North Sea, snow in the air and Mr E J Shaw, Shedmaster at Lynn Loco, in the warmth of his office: never any shortage of coal for the grate there! I was ushered into his office by Driver Jimmy Wood, acting as Running Foreman and based in the outer office. I had heard that Mr Shaw was a hard man to please and that he was a good railwayman trained at Gorton in Manchester by a legendary foreman fitter and breakdown man whose ability Mr Shaw inherited. What had I done, he wanted to know; did I take snuff, was I a beer drinker, did I smoke a pipe, what did I know about Norfolk and Norfolk artisans in particular? They were dead beats, so he said, and he expected me to improve the availability of engines, not an easy job, for Ted Shaw already ran a very tight ship. "You'll be here before eight each morning and see what Gibbons and Cross are up to; you will relieve the night running foreman, make out the engine list for the next day, with washouts and repairs shown. Then I will have to teach you how to do the supplementary list for the engineman, the Sunday list and you will supervise all repair work and assist me to run the shed and yard." This homily was delivered in abrupt and pungent Mancunian in an atmosphere thick with pipe smoke and snuff – thus my introduction to a man whose methods were hard but from whom I learned much about men and running shed life, of economy, and the rostering of enginemen that would stand me in good stead for the rest of my railway life. Till this day, I could still do the King's Lynn duty list with all its twist and turns without a mistake, so durable were Ted Shaw's methods.

In a small office next to the shedmaster worked Reg Herrington, his clerk. He was immensely thorough, would not carry out Mr Shaw's instructions to fiddle the availability returns, had beautiful copperplate writing and was a very good friend to me. His advice was often illuminated by such sayings as "Dick, you can't make a silk purse out of the sow's ear" and "Don't forget, Dick, when dealing with men, attitude is the art of gunnery"! After some months, Reg told me, much to my amazement, that Mr Shaw had reported favourably on me to Cambridge, although he had rightly made a point of my weaknesses. One of these was the fact that I used Christian names when addressing members of his staff and I was sent for by Mr Rees, our District Superintendent, and told that my use of Christian names to the staff must cease as it encouraged familiarity. I thought and still do think that it would be quite wrong for a youngster of 23 to be addressing an engine driver of 64 years of age by his surname and without the 'Mr'. Despite my instructions, I carried on my way for the rest of my railway life and have never regretted it.

The Shedmaster was assisted by two excellent running foremen who came on duty at 4pm one week and midnight the next. These were the rostered times but in fact, informally they changed over at about 9:30pm. This was a sensible arrangement and agreed by the shedmaster before Ted Shaw's time.

Now, let us take a journey from Liverpool St to King's Lynn during the period of trial runs with the new B2 engine, No 1671. I was enjoying a week away from Lynn and acting as part of a small team carrying out the working of two of these locomotives on trial. We arrived on time at Cambridge from Liverpool Street and I waited for the arrival of the second part of this train which was going to be taken forward by one of our D15 locomotives, No 8895. When the train arrived and No 8895 backed on, we learned that we had ten coaches, a hefty load for an old Claud. However, our driver had no qualms; had I been wiser, I would have realised that some mischief was afoot. We started away from Cambridge with Alf Harrington at the regulator. He said that the slide valves were blowing through but the engine should steam pretty well. This proved to be the case and we roared across the Fens towards Ely with the boiler pressure firmly on the red mark of 180 psi. I had asked to do the firing and I had not the slightest trouble with maintaining the boiler, an unusual situation with a D15. So, we duly arrived at Lynn and Alf said that he was going to book the slide valves blowing through.

Now we come to the truth. Alf was a Yorkshireman who had come to Lynn for his fireman's check before the war and who was a considerable character whose universal nickname was 'Satan'. What he had been doing to the engine at Cambridge well before the departure time was to find a long piece of bar and fix it firmly in the smokebox across the blastpipe to act as what was called a 'Jimmy'. Alf had been used to the fearful gradients of the LNER West Riding and he was putting his hard learned lessons into practice. This arrangement was applied to various classes of locomotives, quite illegally but always accepted because it turned a difficult engine into a flyer.

Engine No 8890 was probably the worst of the D15s at King's Lynn and I was determined to improve the steaming somehow. I should say that I was oblivious to the truth of Alf Harrington's performance until years later. So, I arranged for No 8890 to work from King's Lynn to Ely on a Sunday evening so that it would be attached to the 10:15pm from Ely to Lynn. I would be coming back from a weekend at home and catching the train which left London at 7:40pm, not very fast by today's standards but fast enough for my experiments. Briefly, we had a tough time coming from Ely to King's Lynn. Apart from two short gradients, the journey was flat through Littleport to Downham where we stopped and then on to Lynn non-stop.

The No 8890 was a poor old tool and we never had much steam but it went back to about 100 psi on the final gentle rise to St Germans. The water in the boiler was pretty low but we felt that we should make King's Lynn without too much difficulty. As you approach King's Lynn, you are on a left-hand curve and the fireman always looks out for three signals, all of which have to be in the off position. I had never known the third of the three to be at red if we had favourable signals up till then, so to our amazement at this time – 11pm on a Sunday night

TOP RIGHT: Ron Alder and Hector Boot at Marylebone last week of the GC London Extension. Ron and I were at Woodford at the same time. He was then a Fireman and also Chairman of the ASLEF Branch. He was said to be a difficult customer but in fact we had it right from the start, a splendid relationship. In time Ron had to make his mind up whether to go full time with his union or to seek promotion into the management grades. He chose the latter and he chose well because without changing his methods he became a first class manager. The engine is a decrepit Black Five but we coaxed it to Woodford. To sum it up, we had a wonderful time with old colleagues and made our way home on the last train up which I had the pleasure of driving with a good Black Five, Driver George Cave.

BOTTOM RIGHT: Woodford station waiting for the last one up, a few days before closure in 1966. I'm in the centre with the Secretary of the Local Department Committee, Driver George Wootton, and the Chairman, Driver Charlie Sanders, both of whom had retired. What a wonderful pair. Good fighters for what was right and as straight as a table top, therefore we worked in perfect accord.

FAR RIGHT: A rare photograph of a 'Four wheeled Tram' in Lynn Loco for repairs beyond the capability of the little shed at Wisbech. This tram was built in 1897 and preceded the larger J70s which were far more powerful. For all that, my one journey down the 'tram', as it was called, was with this engine, No 7133 and Driver Potter who came from Gorton for a regular driver's job. But No 7133 was also ideally designed for photography. Here we have left-to-right: 'Podmore', who was a mystery man for he worked both as a Boilerwasher and a Shed Labourer and I think a fitter's mate. He was Podmore to everybody, no more no less. Then there is Ted Peck, one of the many railway Pecks at the two sheds, who was a Boilerwasher, and Josh Johnson. He and Ted have done the washing out and Podmore has tagged along.

– this signal was at danger. Driver Alf Birdseye had to make a sharp application of the old fashioned vacuum brake valve and this was too much for No 8890 so we slowed up and stopped by the shed just short of the platform. The signal had cleared before we reached it but despite our efforts to keep going, all this took place within a few feet and much to the amusement of the Running Foreman on duty, Fred Jackson, who was on his way up to the station to find out how things had turned out. Incidentally, Fred Jackson was to become Mayor of King's Lynn in time and I am told that he did an excellent job during his year of office. He was also a very keen Union man and belonged to the RCA which became the present TSSA union. As far as I was concerned, Fred went to endless trouble to coach me on all manner of problems and also he was a shrewd judge of men, an art which he passed on to me for my ultimate benefit.

South Lynn was a very different depot in every way and one felt that the two depots glared at each other across the town. So, we will leave the depot itself for the time being and take a trip down the M&GN, the mainline over which our men worked to Yarmouth Beach, Peterborough and Leicester. It was, to me, a fascinating little place catering for a very hilly road going east and to the west once you were past Bourne. And very different looking enginemen, clean shaven to a man whereas at South Lynn, all manner of distinguished moustaches abounded. At South Lynn, the two running foremen were elderly gentlemen who took matters very easily but the fitting and boiler-making staff were of the highest quality. At King's Lynn there was no 8:00 am shed driver whereas at South Lynn we had the well-known Luke Watson, otherwise known as Rupert, who was about 63, on the 8:00 am regular day turn along with his mate who had never been passed for driving. He was a man of singular ways and more or less ran the shed between 8 and 4 although we kept each other closely informed, so we got on very well and had much in common. He loved to be the oracle and, for example, he would start a conversation about the London and North Eastern Railway as opposed to the M&GN as follows. "My dear Sir, permit me to inform you that the London and North Eastern Railway was noted for laziness and bloody idleness and the Great Eastern was worse!"

Here is one of the incidents that came my way at South Lynn where I was acting shed master for a total about 14 months. Remember that I was very young but I had a considerable degree of success at running the depot. Nevertheless, I was inclined to take risks that a more experienced man would never undertake and some of which brought about my transfer in June 1948 to Headquarters under our great chief, L P Parker. One evening I was in my office which looked out over the shed yard and talking to Arthur Bettinson, our clerk, who was very experienced in that position. We saw a driver approaching and obviously coming to see me so Arthur left me to it. The visitor turned out to be a member of the Local Departmental Committee, the group who represent the footplate staff at the depot

ABOVE: We must now put the clock back to South Lynn because, in spirit, the M&GN, gone these many years, was still around! And it was quite an experience to take charge at the age of 23 of such a fiercely independent shed. So here is one of our South Lynn engines, No 3400, the first of its class built in 1896 for the Great Northern relegated to secondary work long, long ago. We had Driver Jack Thurston and the Fireman was a certain George Edge, not far off being passed for driving at most depots but unlikely at South Lynn. The LMS men wore shiny topped caps but the LNER certainly did not, for theirs were soft and shapely and our GN or GC men wouldn't be seen dead in a Midland cap.

LEFT: So here is a C class rebuild of the M&GN, old No 55 that was, but now that they are on the LNER list where there is already a No 55, the Joint engines are mostly given a duplicate list number – thus No 055. They were splendid engines, with that bit of extra power that was needed for the harder work and capable of hauling prodigious loads in the summer.

and who are elected by the enginemen. This was Les Beales who had had been in the timekeeper's office talking to the driver of the 5:33pm express to Yarmouth. Les told me that the driver, Mo Seaman, was refusing to take the booked engine as it was a very poor steamer and not fit for the job. He also had said to Les that 'Hardy' ought to come with us to see what we have to put up with. So here was Les Beales acting as a go-between saying to me in his persuasive way, "If you go with him, he'd take the engine maybe" and of course I fell into the trap.

Later on, Mo and his mate had brought No 8833 from the shed and out onto the train and I noticed a certain gleam in his eye when he said, "Are you going to fire her, Mr Hardy?" Of course I was and I noticed that when we passed by the shed there were plenty of folk to see us go by. The result was that we had a good start and, although it was my first trip on a Super-Claud, I applied all the practical knowledge I had gained over the years and 8833 came through to Melton Constable with flying colours! But the fact remains that she was not fit for the job and my oppo at Yarmouth Beach put a different engine on the duty for the rest of the week and got to work in the shed on 8833. It is true that, when in charge, you gain a certain respect if you can do the job and I never will forget the wonderful footplate training and experience that came my way.

The Local Departmental Committe (LDC) at South Lynn was excellent and straight and they were prepared to help wherever possible, Ernie Drew, Bill Pooley (who came to my wedding in 1949) and Les Beales. When it came to the 44 hour week, quite unheard of amongst enginemen, we got our heads together and sitting in the Pooleys' front room on a Sunday, supplied the finishing touches to our enginemen's rosters. They came into being about a fortnight later and worked like a charm although it was easier if the crews were in links of twelve or, at the bigger depots, there were 36 or 24 turn rosters, as in the Britannia link of 36 turns at Stratford. If there was any trouble brewing, one of the three would come and tip me off and as often as not, there was a ready and practical answer to the problem and the perpetrator would be satisfied with no hassle on either side.

And now a typical railway manoeuvre of the past which happened in the old days. It was a terrible night, mid-winter, with the coldest of winds and Luke Watson and his mate Bill Pooley took duty punctually in the early hours. Bill was in his 20s and Rupert about 45 years of age. Luke told his mate to all but close the damper and fill the firebox with coal to the very brim! In the meantime he went in search of a decent sized plank to rest across the cab between the splashers which would be a warm seat heated by a fire which, by now, was really alight. They fixed the overhead storm-sheets above the footplate, let the sides down and, quietly, away they went off the shed to find their train in the yard. Most of the signal boxes were switched out and then their road was set, a pop on the whistle and gently away towards Sutton Bridge, a vile night and difficult to see but Rupert and his mate set the engine to reach about 15–20 mph, opened the firehole doors and sat

RIGHT: A dull Sunday morning in 1951 and 1535, one of the Ipswich B12s has been washed out, the fire lit and hauled out of the shed (which held four engines out of 91) to be cleaned and polished, although the paintwork was unlined black and rough at that. It gives you an idea of the working conditions of those days. Soon one of the cleaners will go up a ladder to stand on the handrail, leaning forward to do the top of the boiler. He stays the right side of the vertical – or else – which never happened in my experience. On the left is Tammy Gooch, Chargehand Cleaner, an ex driver who had failed, as so many did with poor colour vision: he died suddenly in 1952. As he is a cleaner short of the usual four, he is doing his bit. Those 16-year-old cleaners probably started straight from school in 1950 and none of them expected to be photographed, yet look at their dress. Being a cleaner was a dirty job and yet all three sport a collar and tie. They will be in their mid-eighties by now. Young Rayner stands nearest to the camera but the names of the other boys have gone, nor did I see any of them grow to manhood. The 3:35pm will go up to London with the 6:00pm and come back with the Norwich mail, a tough job for a B12. But her crew will make light of it: Drivers Jim Calver and Charlie Parr and their firemen worshipped their old engine and her footplate was like a jeweller's shop, everything burnished. They took a pride that could never be measured in cold figures but worth so very much.

together on the plank warm as toast in front of that great fire. The engine was, an old M&GN Johnson six coupled goods. They knew perfectly well when Sutton Bridge was getting nearer and where they would resume their normal positions and sharp look-out. That is the way it was, perfectly thought out and impossible to see ahead but the driver, fireman and guard knew the road blindfold and so the first stage of the job was done. But you would never have committed this sort of thing to paper nor even talked about it.

So, in September 1949, L P Parker directed me to take charge at Woodford in Northants but only ten miles from Banbury. We had 50 engines, B17 and V2s for the passenger and fitted freight work, WD Austerities for the heavy and fast freight jobs to Neasden with some excellent craftsmen to maintain the fleet, but terrible water so that the boilers and fireboxes needed constant attention.

Gwenda and I were truly happy in our little cottage in the village of Eydon near Woodford and then without warning, in July 1950, I was whisked off to East Anglia by the all-powerful L P Parker. My boss, equally surprised, had a word with L P Parker who said that "If Hardy doesn't go to Ipswich, he won't go anywhere for a very long time." Much to my amazement, I was appointed Shedmaster four days later. Ipswich was said to be a handful and, in some ways, it was but the Suffolkers were very good railwaymen. The original depot dated back to the 1840s but the main part came a little later. We had 91 engines, coaled by hand by coalmen standing on the top of coal wagons or shovelling out of the side door on a trestle.

The leading fitter and leading boilermaker had an office near mine as well as to the mechanical foreman. Put in a nutshell, their grasp of everything was unassailable. Also in the office was a character by the name of Claud Sansom who was known as the Shop Officeman. His background was totally different to the others who were trained as craftsmen, fitters and boilermakers and he came to Ipswich from Gorton, Manchester in the 1930s as a driver and a very good one he became after he had learned the roads. Right through the War he was driving and his great disappointment was that, after war was declared, lodging turns were abolished and so Ipswich lost their Manchester lodge job which they had had since 1927, lodging in Gorton and returning to Ipswich the next day via Sheffield Victoria, Retford, Lincoln, March, home to Ipswich via Ely, Bury St Edmunds, and Stowmarket. As the ex-LMS officers were appointed to the senior posts at Headquarters, so they brought with them the LMS systems which meant far more paperwork than we of the LNER needed to record the same information but Claud revelled in the job and tackled all the various problems successfully, if with a considerable amount of backchat.

Jack Percy and Charlie Winney were the two Chargemen who did a remarkable job. Jack had a vast knowledge of engine maintenance and his fitting staff respected him completely. Nevertheless, he was occasionally baffled by the

LEFT: Ipswich station in the 1950s, tight for room but a well-managed station where staff were efficient. Station staff with a lot to load in a two minute stop would keep one eye on their task and the other on the engine. If taking water when they were loaded, any more time over two minutes went to 'loco'. But this train is an up Yarmouth and changing engines: the fireman has unhooked and when he is back on the engine away they go to the shed. The starting signal will be replaced and the Norwich 7MT off 095am to Ipswich will come forward and work the train to London.

way a certain locomotive was behaving. Charlie did not have Jack's unflappable temperament but to hear an explosion from him over something that was trying his patience signified that Charlie had found signs of something radically wrong with a boiler or firebox but that it would be put right quickly and effectively. I have never known boilers kept in such perfect condition as they were at Ipswich. When I moved on to Stewarts Lane, Charlie came up to see me for a day out and found that matters on the Southern were handled in a manner that did not suit him at all!

But there were about 480 people employed at our depot in Ipswich and on the whole, the shed, although dating back to mid-Victorian times and being hopelessly outdated, was extremely well run by the considerable number of men in various jobs working around the clock. So the engines were well looked after whether they were mainline, goods or shunting engines and most of the Enginemen were well satisfied, particularly those who had a share in the operation of a regular engine. On the other hand, the coaling of the engines was completely outdated but it had to meet our requirements and we had a mechanical digger of great age which picked up coal from the ground but it was a pretty unreliable piece of machinery. So the coalmen on shifts coaled the tenders of the engines with either their own hands or with pick and shovel. They stood to do this either on top of the coal or on the open door resting on a trestle and shovelled upwards and into the engine's bunker or tender over the coalman's shoulder. Hard work but it was done.

I have referred to regular manning of engines and how the engineman's whole life seemed to revolve around the engine allocated to them. There was No 1059, the B1 driven by Frank Cocksedge and Jim Calver and aided by their regular firemen, who got top class performance from their engine. But then all the other men in the link would disagree vigorously with that point of view. For example, there was Charlie Parr who ran a B12 No 1535, to which he referred as 'Old 35'. On a Sunday, when he was booked to work a train leaving Ipswich in the late afternoon, he would be seen stumping towards the running foreman's office about noontime. Immediately as he found the foreman, he would ask the same question "Have I got my old gal tonight, foreman?" "Yes Charlie, you've got 'Old 35', she's been washed out and in good form." "That'll do, then," Charlie said, and off he would stump back home to have his dinner. This is just but one example of the pride that men took in their work once they had been given a nominated engine.

There were many other grades of staff down to the Shed Labourers who kept the shed and yard at Ipswich as clean as it was possible to do and on a Sunday, where a great deal of maintenance had to be carried out, the ash wagons and their shunting engine were going hither and thither trying to keep out of the way as they loaded heaps of ash. But nowhere else did I ever come across another Jack Finch, who came to my retirement party, much to my amazement, at BR Headquarters. But it did my heart good to see him again. Jack moved to Norwich

RIGHT: LNER poster advertising weekly holiday season tickets, Eastern Counties (Area No 5).

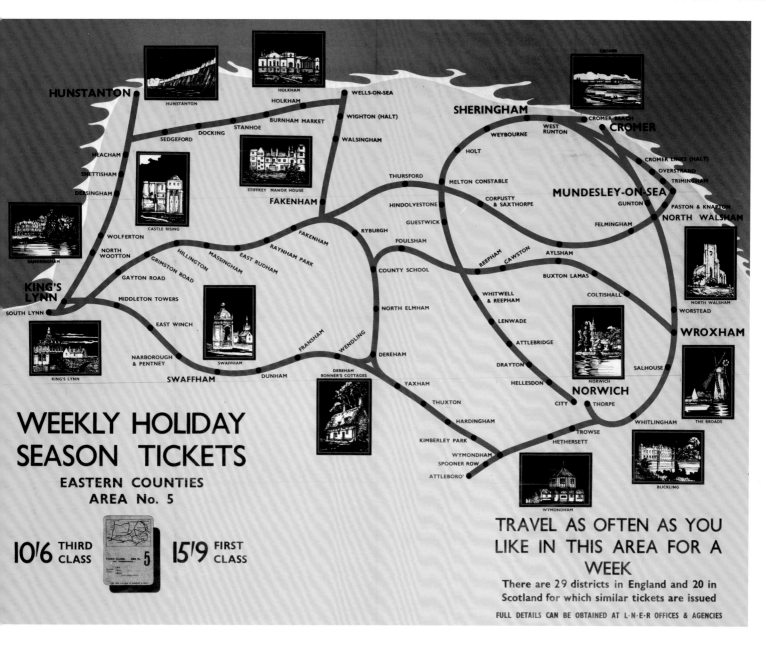

WEEKLY HOLIDAY SEASON TICKETS

EASTERN COUNTIES AREA No. 5

10/6 THIRD CLASS

15/9 FIRST CLASS

TRAVEL AS OFTEN AS YOU LIKE IN THIS AREA FOR A WEEK

There are 29 districts in England and 20 in Scotland for which similar tickets are issued

FULL DETAILS CAN BE OBTAINED AT L·N·E·R OFFICES & AGENCIES

after my time, as Chargehand Engine Cleaner, and no doubt he made a wonderful job of whatever he was required to do. But at Ipswich, on paper, he was a shed labourer though in practice he would cover any job that came his way. However, there was one which he regarded solely as his own. In our old depot, the drains went back to the dark ages and there was only one man in any department, never mind ours, who could deal with serious flooding or some such thing in Ipswich Loco. There was no paperwork, but he would not share his knowledge with anybody else as he treasured the overtime and night work payments that came his way when the foreman said, "Send for Jack Finch", and Jack would arrive in no time in his standard uniform of an old army officer's tunic, overall trousers, bike clips, a cloth cap tilted jauntily and a determined expression when he got to work. Jack was one of the best.

We have already talked about the LDCs at South Lynn but I was very fortunate wherever I went to find that the staff were represented by men who were masters of their own jobs, trustworthy and capable of grasping the complexities of my job, as well as supporting successfully the men that they represented. The Chairman was Fred Thorpe who was a senior Driver on his regular and much vaunted No 1566. He had had been in France during the First World War having joined the newly formed branch of the Royal Engineers, the Railway Operating Division. He had been a keen young fireman at Ipswich and gained priceless experience working in France. Fred was abrupt and spoke his mind but he was an excellent chairman. His secretary was Ernie Payne, who I came to know very well indeed. He was in the top link and his engine was a B1 No 1201 and he went to a great deal of trouble to keep his engine maintained to the highest level. Ernie had a remarkable career. He joined the Great Eastern Railway in about 1912 and joined up pretty early in the War, long before the ROD had been formed. Therefore he was not connected with railways and ultimately he found that he had the opportunity to join the Royal Flying Corps as a Captain and he was training to become a pilot when the War came to an end. In due course he returned to Ipswich and the railway and became a tip-top fireman who was selected, along with Driver George Pinkney, to work the first Manchester lodge turn in 1927 with the B12 No 8535 and he became Major Payne, Officer commanding the Railway Home Guard, Ipswich, in the last one! The third member of the LDC was Arthur Brooks who was in the mainline goods link. Arthur had his own comical and rather grand way of expressing himself and was also very good at pouring oil on troubled waters. And finally, there was a fourth man who was also on the photograph, called Bert Coleman, who represented the shed grades such as the boiler washers, time keepers, coalmen and also a great variety of staff in what were called the Conciliation Grades. Bert had done every job in the depot bar Jack Finch's but including cover at the various outposts such as relieving 'Down the Tram' and was first class at all of them.

RIGHT: This is Thursford on the M&GN main line heading for Yarmouth and the end of the train is almost out of sight. The engine is a J17 with 4ft 10ins, six coupled driving wheels, built with the steam brake only but selected as an engine suitable for fitting with the vacuum brake for hauling fitted stock.

LEFT: No 8881 was a half-decent D15 'Claud', one of the King's Lynn allocation and back from Stratford Works after a general overhaul. Our other D15s were Nos 8890, 8891, 8893, 8895 with 8896 at Hunstanton until the Royal Claud 8783 arrived in early spring 1946. On the left is 'Laddy' Bridges, one of the senior passed firemen, at 45, still not a regular driver though not far off. Then Driver Jimmy Woods, who was a Cockney and Secretary of the Mutual Improvement Class. He also acted as running foreman as required and was on duty and showed me into Ted Shaw's office the day that I arrived. Like 'Laddy', he was a splendid railwayman. Next is the perennial Syd Joplin, and finally John Cook who had been a South Lynn fireman passed for driving and sadly had to come off the footplate and was transferred to King's Lynn.

ABOVE RIGHT: The South Lynn Improvement Class – part of a countrywide voluntary group run by enginemen to improve their knowledge of all aspect of locomotive design and performance, as well as rules and regulations – had an annual outing to the Science Museum in London. The author knew many of the men in the photograph who were all engine drivers or firemen at South Lynn on the M&GN section of the LNER.

RIGHT: A very quiet spell on a March Saturday when I was learning the Running Foreman's job on afternoons. "Time for a photo," said Stan Bowers, the Foreman in the trilby and we went outside the little office and stores block and the two men sat on the sleepers near to the turntable. In fact, this was the makeshift buffer stop used if an engine overshot the table. There is not an engine in sight, nothing outside the 'Royal' carriage shed on the down side. Stan gave the picture its name, 'Five minutes after the bomb fell'. Syd Joplin was the 8–4 Timekeeper always wearing a species of bow tie and real old-fashioned country corduroy trousers. We shared the office with the running foreman on duty. Stan was typically dressed for the part: we were not a bowler hat railway, the GE nor the M&GN come to that.

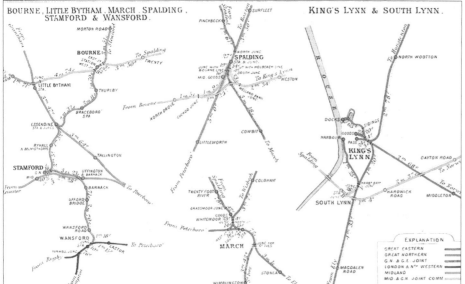

BOURNE, LITTLE BYTHAM, MARCH, SPALDING, STAMFORD & WANSFORD.

KING'S LYNN & SOUTH LYNN.

ABOVE: The purple lines are the the old GER and the yellow lines are the M&GN Joint. In 1946–8, the lines were as shown here in 1915, although Hardwick Road station had gone by then. The Docks and Harbour branches in practice seemed a complicated maze, but not so on the map. Shunting engines were hard at work during weekdays.

The three main lines out to Hunstanton, Dereham and Ely are noted and well-used in the summer especially. The M&GN was closed in 1959, well before the Beeching era, and the general manager of the Eastern Region took the decision to close, as was his right. The bridge over the Ouse was known as West Lynn Bridge and the yards were a hive of activity on weekdays. As for the summer in peacetime, with the railway largely single line and heavily graded, miracles of haulage by out-dated M&GN locomotives were performed as a matter of routine.

RIGHT: Over the Great Ouse River and a 10mph speed is in order. A pick up goods perhaps but not a lot of business. The road is set for the yard and he will have a nice steady little run down the short bank into South Lynn. Again these little engines may well have worked passenger trains at the weekends and No 084 is a J4 and a free running engine and even though a small boiler freight engine, when there are heavy loads to be handled, she will let-fly and so will the rockets and maybe the line side farmers will have something to say.

ABOVE: This is the author in 1947 and this time on the footplate of an oil-fired Austerity where you will see me lighting up (for the benefit of the local newspaper). This is the only time that I travelled from Ely on an old J15 to the outskirts of Cambridge at Barnwell Junction where I was able to walk back to my temporary digs.

ABOVE RIGHT: Before my day, probably in the mid-1930s, but there is one thing certain and that it is a C-class engine, No 38, unrebuilt, that it is leaving South Lynn and working hard up the rise over the Great Eastern mainline to Ely. This engine ultimately became No 038 and was withdrawn from service in September 1943. Look at the tender, and it will tell you that the driver and fireman have taken as much coal onto the tender as is more or less safe and by the look of the engine's exhaust, they will get through quite a pile by the time they get to Melton Constable.

ABOVE LEFT: Here is a lovely photo, full of interest: although not marked I think that this picture is at Yarmouth Beach. This is a D52 leaving the terminus from the down side platform. The D52 has that remarkably large chimney which looks like a GW affair on a small boiler but the dome still has its Salter valves and the rear safety valve with its cover going back to S W Johnson's day.

ABOVE RIGHT: Yarmouth Beach Station and a train is shortly to leave, probably on its way westward to Melton Constable and taking its time because it is a stopping train over a heavy road. Certainly it has a standard G6 Belpaire boiler. The engine's features such as the chimney and dome are of Midland design but the cab is of no known design and at first I felt that it had a touch of Great Northern about it. Only a few of these engines were built.

TOP LEFT: A Sunday morning in June 1952 in Ipswich Loco. In the background the Running Shed which held four of the 91 allocated No 1253, class B1 is standing on the short pit and has just been washed out. It will be lit up, cleaned and then work an evening job to London.

From the left: Arthur Rumbellow ('Rummy'), Running Foreman, a likeable man but a very laid back foreman; Fred Locksmith, Shed Turner, an excellent if fiery man. In times of stress, Fred was given to throwing his shunting pole on the ground and stamping on it. Jack Baldwin, Rummy's No 2, was a very able man, also rather laid back, which did not always suit me. He left the railway long before his time. Harold Alen, NCT (Non-Clerical Timekeeper) and captain of the Ipswich Loco Cricket XI for which I used to play. When Rummy was a driver, he was instructed by the foreman to take a J15 Black Goods with the breakdown vans through to the station where there had been a derailment in the yard. The engine was standing ready and the fireman should have checked the condition of his fire. On the way, however, the steam pressure began to fall and Rummy, with his pipe stuck upwards in his mouth, said to his fireman, "I should have a look at that fire, old mate, if I was you." This he did rather unwillingly to discover a completely empty firebox. They reached the station with a struggle and got lit up with a bit of fire from another engine and some wood from somewhere.

TOP RIGHT: No 65447 ran the Mid-Suffolk Railway, whose little shed came under Ipswich where I was Shedmaster. She is standing at Kenton down home signal at danger as it had been out of use for many months, although this was far from common knowledge. The crossing gates are across the line so the driver had stopped at the signal. In the winter of 1950–51, I caught the mid-morning train from Haughley for Laxfield. I travelled with the driver-in-charge at Laxfield, George Rouse, who spoke in the broad Yorkshire tones of Barnsley. In the late 1920s when times were hard in the north, it seemed to George that he would never be made a driver at Barnsley so he put in for driving jobs in the south and turned up at Laxfield where he and his wife and family lived happily. On the day I travelled, George drew up at Kenton home signal and sounded the whistle imperiously. The gates were across the road and clear for us but nothing happened until the porter in charge suddenly appeared and waved the train past the signal. George, however, did not move and blew the whistle again: the porter re-appeared in a fury with a green flag and waved the train forward and into the platform. I stood well back against the firebox whilst listening to the porter bawling out the driver who with nods and winks made it clear that he had the boss with him and to keep his mouth shut. The standard drill was to stop at the signal if the gates were closed (as in the picture). I decided not to re-write the MSLR personal rule book. Doctor Ian Allen who took the photo was George's family doctor!

BOTTOM: No 5467, and it is a J15. It is a good many years since I saw a weed-killing train but here is one and the spray can be seen at work. We provided the engine for the civil engineer: plenty of branch lines in Suffolk. The driver was 'Skit' Eley from Ipswich and the train is between Wickham Market and Framlingham.

LEFT: A Framlingham–Liverpool St excursion stopping at Hacheston Halt to pick up passengers for London. The guard will get off, get the step ladder, help passengers aboard, hoist up the ladder and away they go to Wickham Market and all points south. The engine is D16/3 2552 and is worked throughout by Ipswich men.

ABOVE: No 70000, *Britannia*, the first 7MT making its first journey to Norwich with the down Norfolkman. Driver Bill Redhead of Stratford is accompanied by Chief Inspector Len Theobald. I'm standing between the 'uprights' to wish them well on their journey.

TOP RIGHT: 'Worth Your While – Worthwhile Jobs on British Railways'. Poster produced in 1951 for BR London Midland Region to advertise employment vacancies for porters, drivers, checkers and capstanmen, detailing staff benefits and minimum rates of pay. Artwork by an unknown artist.

ABOVE: Here is No 34059 *Sir Archibald Sinclair* at Parkeston Quay in 1949 when she was on trial. The Railway Executive intended to transfer what they considered to be under-used light Pacifics from West Country to the GE section based at Stratford and Norwich. Our chief, L P Parker, was a party to plans for an entirely new high-speed timetable using what he hoped would be the class 7 BR standard then on the drawing board. In no circumstances would he have any Bulleids at Stratford on a permanent basis, although the engine distinguished itself on trial with a picked crew and Chief Inspector Len Theobald in attendance. From the left: HQ Inspector Tom Sands, ex M&GN who retired as Chief Inspector, Norwich; Driver Bill Burritt of Stratford and his regular mate who later moved to Gorton; Len Theobald, an outstanding Chief Inspector for whom L P Parker had great respect.

ABOVE: Early morning rush hour at Liverpool St station, London, 12 October 1951. This station was the busiest terminus in London at this time. During the 1940s lines into the station were electrified to provide a more efficient and faster service, although the station was still very crowded at peak times.

RIGHT: Ipswich, June 1952, north end of the running shed. No 1634 *Hinchingbrooke* had just been washed out, examined with great care by Charlie Ransom, boilermaker, as his chargehand Charlie Winney demanded the highest standards of workmanship. From left: Maury Smith, the giant Boilerwasher; Jack Reed and Charlie Ransom, Boilermakers; and the little Tube Cleaner, Billy Rudd. All four were first class men at their job. Sunday was a very busy day in Ipswich depot with so many engines requiring attention and with little or no room in which to do the necessary repairs.

FAR LEFT: Where else but the 'Middy'? First down train of the day over the Mid-Suffolk Light Railway leaves Haughley for Laxfield and climbs the 1 in 42 gradient, with a few passengers and some freight, Ipswich driver Ernie Baker and Ron Thompson of Laxfield. A wonderful East Anglian scene: J15 No 5447, the regular engine for the Mid-Suffolk by 1952.

LEFT: Old Ipswich! The 'Tram Road' with a 'tram' in for repairs. The excellent breakdown crane, water tank and oil stores are in evidence, as is the fitting shop and the 'wagon wheels shunt'. The carriage and wagon shunter is hitching a ride on the J15 No 5382 on her last legs. The driver is Bill Mutimer.

RIGHT: Pigg's Grave summit near Melton Constable. No 2509 class D15 has brought 11 Midland bogies up five miles, 1 in 100. In 1950, the Clauds were well past their best which makes the work of the M&GN crew so creditable, but those men were used to small engines with heavy loads.

LEFT: An unusual photograph, taken by a certain Jimmy James, an Ipswich schoolmaster who frequently visited us with his most interested charges or with his friends to see what we got up to at Ipswich Loco on a Sunday morning. So far so good but we had been recently instructed to prepare one of our B1s for an exhibition in or near Norwich which we were delighted to arrange. Why Norwich were not given the task or why they had so little to say about it, I never tried to find out, indeed one kept one's mouth shut and got on with the job. Our B1s were in excellent condition and as all but two (1054 and 1056) were booked to their own sets of driver and fireman, we had plenty to choose from. Certainly through most of 1952, No 1059 was in a class of her own, operated by her two nominated drivers with firemen cleaning and burnishing everything that could be given the works. From front to rear buffers and, of course, there was endless copper, steel and brass work to be polished. No doubt the normal engine cleaners might well lend a hand for there could be quite a few youths on duty who might be needed as firemen later in the morning.

No 1059 had its cab roof or 'hood' painted cream which in the intense firelight lit up beautifully all the burnished brass, copper and steelwork in the cab. Soon drivers were coming to see me about having their 'hood done' and the aforesaid Fred Thorpe wanted to know bluntly why Cocksedge and Calver's engine had been done and not his. All good for pride in the job and Fred had his done the following week. But by lunch time, No 1059 looked marvellous and by and by away she went to Norwich. The exhibition was a success and I believe Norwich played their part to the full.

But when was the photo taken and who are the members of the staff? Jimmy James had probably asked if he could take a photograph of the staff and Jack Percy the Leading Fitter on the right of the picture, would have got his staff that had worked on the engine together. A few of them are still alive and it is to be hoped that they have a copy of the photograph. I remember most of the men for as shedmaster, one aims to know every member of one's staff in time. As I have said, there were 480 men and boys (and two ladies) working at Ipswich Loco and it is great to look back and remember the Ipswich staff and recall and read again the many letters that I have kept, from men who have made my life so full of human interest.

STEWARTS LANE DEPOT AND THE

STRATFORD

DISTRICT

1952–1962

05

Stewarts Lane will never be forgotten by me and a host of us still are on the go. It was a blessing that I made a reply to the advertisement to apply for the job. While I was waiting to be interviewed at Waterloo by Mr Chrimes, the Southern Motive Power Superintendent, I was listening to the advice of George Weeden, once of the Eastern, that, on the Southern, you must never forget that trains must run on time. Everybody was accountable, shedmasters, stationmasters, Control themselves, signalmen, guards, PW and S&T departments and so far as the Motive Power Dept was concerned, there was a 'League table' for time lost per thousand miles run. I was accountable for all time lost by Stewarts Lane men and engines. Sometimes the time was shown on the lost time ticket, sometimes the ticket found its way onto my desk and at Stew Lane, John Greenfield, a grade four clerk, was imbued with the same spirit and kept me posted on every detail and travelled up from Goring-by-Sea every weekday! He loved his job, indeed he was passionate that our depot must be at the top of the list. In fact, it never was because of the number of very heavy empty stock trains that had to tackle heavy gradients on their way to such places as Eardley sidings in the Streatham area. At the head of the train, an H class tank, manful little engines which rarely if ever stuck on Grosvenor Road bank for the banker did his job especially if the driver was the likes of 'Spindle' Morley of happy memory. But only as far as the second overbridge out of Victoria at the foot of the 1 in 64 incline. Then there was Tulse Hill bank up from Herne Hill, much of it at 1 in 78. Now and again, a train would stick on the bank or be stopped halfway up and then out would shoot the Herne Hill Sidings shunting engine, always an E2 (ex-LBSC) engine, also a good 'un, on his way to render assistance and then drop down again to HH to get on with the shunting. Or the next electric up the bank could be told to do the job if he was around. Time mattered to everybody and all classes of work including freight jobs: just as it should be.

And here is an example, on a Monday, early evening in high summer 1954. Driver Bert Hutton and Fireman Peter Morley of SL lost two minutes up the bank from Folkestone to Sandling but was right time through Tonbridge. On my desk on the Tuesday there was the lost time ticket with an explanation of sorts. We knew Bert as a very 'light' driver and it would have been dealt with verbally by John Greenfield. But also on the desk was a wire to say that some SNCF senior officers were travelling on the same train on the Tuesday. The Superintendent of the line, S W Smart, and his party was also travelling so I decided later in the day, to go down to Folkestone Junction myself, as our Inspector was already out on a job. I joined Bert and his mate, we dealt with Monday's lost time, I said that I would like a spell of firing and away we went with a Battle of Britain Bulleid, No 34071. We were running comfortably a shade before time through Tonbridge and set about the bank up to the Sevenoaks tunnel. Clear road through Hildenborough but the Weald box had his distant on and we were climbing at 1 in 122 with 12 coaches and two vans. So Bert kept her going at the same speed and when we passed the distant, it was still at caution but Bert and his mate immediately turned their heads and were rewarded by the signalman's 'late pull' so we simply kept going at the same speed, a good piece of railway work.

Eventually we arrived at Victoria a couple of minutes before time. The three of us got off the engine. It was a warm evening, and we watched what we could see of the passing throng. Mr Smart and his Frenchman were making for cars in the centre road of the station when the Superintendent of the line broke away from his guests and made a bee-line for the engine. He was a little man and a wonderful railwayman but he didn't know any of us on the engine, for we were not in his department, so he opened the conversation "Well done Driver, well done Fireman". Then he turned to me and looked me up and down and said, "Well, who are you then?" and I replied, "I'm Hardy, the Shedmaster at Stewarts Lane and this is one of our best engines." And, warming to the subject, I told him about the incident at the Weald signal box and about the 'late pull' and he came close and put his hand on my shoulder saying, "Capital, boy, capital, that's what I like to see, real railway work"! That made us feel ten foot tall!

I have been in correspondence recently with the Atlantic Group at Sheffield Park and making a comparison between the original Atlantic Class engine on the Great Northern Railway and the Brighton Atlantics. I was able to travel on No 2424 only a relatively short distance but, having done hundreds of miles on the Great Northern Atlantics, the comparison was both rewarding and extremely interesting. I have found some notes written by Philip Evetts back in 1951, which were given to me many years ago, and I convinced myself that I had got to the bottom of the driver's age-old seating arrangements on the Newhaven Atlantics. An entirely unofficial modification enabled the driver to be seated at his work although the problem was not completely solved. As designed, there were no seats on the driver's side because there was no room to rig up the conventional hinged wooden seat as all available room was occupied by the firebox front and the air operated reversing gear which also had a screw reverser for hand adjustment to the rear of the air gear and near the left hand cab doors.

Whoever was in charge of Newhaven shed approached the marine people and between them they designed and concocted a species of saddle resting on the sizeable air brake casting and slotted down the middle lengthways so that the driver could see the figures on his reversing gear rack and the position of the indicator. For all that, he had to get up to peer through the slot and operate the controls. So now the driver could ride his 'saddle' astride until he needed to alter the cut-off or ride side-saddle with his legs dangling or sit side-saddle, slide off and do the whole operation from a standing position before resuming his side-saddle posture. No wonder that the enginemen used to go miles at the same cut-off and all adjustments to power output made by means of the regulator.

TOP LEFT: This photograph was taken in 1956 or so by Dr Ian Allen, who was being looked after by Dick Elmer, Loco Inspector, who used to say, "I wonder where Dr Allen will take me today?" This was a regular occurrence enjoyed by both participants as they were both humorous people and also extremely good at their respective professions. On the other hand, it is doubtful if a visitor to such a depot today would be allowed on the premises but this was all but 60 years ago. The geography is worth noting for you have the background of Stratford Works 'over the uvverside', our own crane shop is visible next to the running lines and the foreground is all part of the new shed (built in 1871).

MIDDLE LEFT: We had three of these engines in my time at Stratford and they had a wonderful reputation on the London, Tilbury and Southend section and having sampled them myself with a Stratford driver and fireman who had spent some years on the LTS, I agree that they were capable of excellent work. It was the injectors that the Southend men detested and where there were several stationed and at an ASLEF branch meeting, the men agreed to notify the local management that they would refuse to take them out of the shed or to do any work on the main line with them. Our District Motive Power Superintendent at Stratford was TCB Miller and I was his assistant and I well remember coming back from lunch in the Broadway with TCB and passing one of the LTS engines whereupon he said, "Hardy, we have got to do something about these engines."

BOTTOM LEFT: Stratford Loco Jubilee Shed on Tender side; these J15s were always known by their nickname of 'Westo Goods'. Much has been written about these little engines as one of them has been preserved, but, provided they were very carefully fired, they would take quite heavy loads and I remember in my first burst at Stratford in 1945 that there was always a heavy passenger train that ran on a Saturday straight through to Maldon. Only light locomotives were allowed on the branch from Witham so the train engine throughout was a J15 and they did a noble job.

However, through the kindness of Fred Rich and Fred Bailey, I am now in possession of a photograph taken on one of the later Atlantics and I think that my assumption of the driver sitting bestride the reversing gear could be wrong. I think that there is insufficient room for the driver's left leg to fit between the new seat and the side of the cab so there it is, and all I can say is the Brighton Atlantics were wonderful engines and they did top class work right up until the end, but they were even more uncomfortable to work on than the Great Northern engines, which were bad enough. It seems from reading the articles, that the Brighton Atlantics rode pretty smoothly whereas the GN engines were very wild riding machines, as I well know from my own experience.

I made but one journey on No 2424, from Victoria to Croydon, where I had to leave the engine, but I had made my first trip and greatly enjoyed the experience, so like the original engine and yet in so many details, quite different. It is a real experience to visit Sheffield Park and see the progress made with No 2424 and one day, she will take the road from Sheffield Park up to East Grinstead and I would love to see her making light work of the heavy gradients of the Bluebell.

Almost invariably, in my time, the well-known Uckfield job which left Victoria at 6:10pm was worked by a Newhaven engine and Stewarts Lane men, a situation that displeased the Newhaven men and also Phillip Evetts, who travelled regularly in the first coach behind the engine. No doubt, when nobody was about, that he was spirited onto the footplate, and I heard not long ago that he lived to a very great age. The normal engine was what we called a 'Fairburn Tank'; neither Newhaven nor Stewarts Lane reckoned much to the performance of these engines, especially the injectors which were at times pretty unreliable. But now and again, an Atlantic would come up on Duty 742. After the engine had arrived in London, it came to Stewarts Lane and then in the afternoon, brought the empty coaches up from Eardley Sidings for the 5:50pm Victoria to Tunbridge Wells West. A change of crews took place just before 6pm and on my trip we had driver, Tom Simmonds, who was well acquainted with the Atlantics. I remember that he perched himself, for he was a smallish man, in his left hand corner and away we went. I was going to fire the engine to Croydon and had made preparations to have a good, big fire, well burnt through and particularly filling the back corners of the grate. In other words, exactly like the GN engines. On the other hand, the driver was on left instead of the right and, as I have never fired from the right-hand side of the cab, I decided not to try but nevertheless to keep out of the driver's way. But the direction of my coal had to be accurate, which meant my wrists were very much more involved than if I had fired correctly from the right hand side and I was standing centrally rather than from than the right. Still we got there in reasonable form and everything was in apple-pie order for their departure.

Now, back in 1927, the first of a new class of engine had been allocated to Battersea shed for trial running with the boat trains normally very heavily loaded. The engine was No 850, named *Lord Nelson,* and she was booked to Driver Stuckey and Fireman Tom Banton. That well-known recorder of locomotive performance, Cecil J Allen, was to travel in the cab to watch the working and so Tom's handling of the shovel was to the highest order and he was thoroughly enjoying himself. So the run was well written up in the *Railway Magazine.* In time, Tom was passed for driving and Battersea had been renamed 'Stewarts Lane' and now he was an excellent driver and mate in the Top Link when a certain incident took place which involved us both.

In 1954, Tom and his mate, Denis Smith, were booked to work the *Golden Arrow* to Folkestone and up from Dover for a week, on duty 12:35pm for 1:35pm off the shed and light engine to Victoria and depart for Folkestone Junction. The engine regularly booked on this job was the famous No 70004, *William Shakespeare,* always cleaned and polished to the highest standards as befitted the engine hauling such an important train. I used to see the engine away from the shed with everything in perfect order but on one occasion, I arrived at the last moment to find that the engine had slipped round for coal and No 70004's safety valves had lifted, showering the spotless engine with coal dust and dirt. This was quite unnecessary and I told Tom so in no uncertain manner, in fact we had very strong words before he pushed off to Victoria in very high dudgeon to work his train. Next day when I saw him take duty, I bade him good morning but he completely ignored me. Stewarts Lane was a pretty tough depot where folk spoke their mind but rarely carried a grudge so I let it be and so things remained for several weeks, still cutting me dead.

One afternoon, a week or two later, I decided to go across to Cannon St and refresh my knowledge of the roads there and also at the eastern side of London Bridge. I also decided to travel down to Faversham and back with our men and a Stewarts Lane engine coming home. As I set off, I asked the list clerk who was the driver on the 4:45pm down: he looked and replied "Tommy Banton"! But I went just the same, arrived at Cannon St, walked down the train up to the engine. Quietly, I got up onto the footplate and said, "I'm coming with you, Tom, and here is my pass." No reply so, after passing London Bridge and the signals ahead all in our favour, I said to Dick Marsh, the Fireman and an excellent ex-Navy man, "Sit you down, Dick, and I'll give you a blow to Chatham." So I started firing and I noticed that we were accelerating pretty quickly and we went through Grove Park with the engine throwing fire and my firing having to be continuous. Of course Tom was in pole position, to 'kill me stone dead.' So up through Elmstead Woods bank we went, Tom completely absorbed with his revenge for he had me completely in his grasp. Chislehurst and near the top, we swung across pretty fast at the junction with the old Chatham & Dover line from Victoria. So now Tom set sail like a bat out of hell and thrashed the engine wherever he could, utterly absorbed in making my life very hard. Anyhow he had to coast down the five miles

RIGHT: Liverpool St No 11 platform and a Norwich Britannia No 70007 at the head of a down Clacton Express on a Saturday afternoon. The photograph was taken in about 1960 by Dr Ian Allen who was about to travel on the footplate to Colchester. Ian knew an enormous number of railwaymen and was much liked so he got a splendid reception from the driver and fireman and the Locomotive Inspector travelling on the footplate. I think that I travelled with them as far as Chelmsford because I now recall Ron Eagle offered me the regulator as we passed Stratford. I accepted with the greatest of pleasure. Ernie Foskett who stands in the middle of the group, was the acting Inspector and he hopped in the train whilst I was there so we did not exceed four people on the engine. The Fireman on the left is Len Cutmore and he and Ron Eagle were Clacton men. We did have a perfect trip and all of us played our part and I was sorry to have to leave them at Chelmsford. My place was taken by Ernie Foskett, who would then look after Dr Ian Allen.

of Sole Street bank and, passing Chatham, I said to Dick Marsh that I had better finish the job so Tom thrashed the engine and did his best to get me to cry for mercy but no, and we eventually arrived at Faversham, well before time, where our relief was waiting. So Tom and his mate climbed down, followed by myself. I laughed: "Are you feeling better now, Tom? And he replied, "Yes, Guv'nor. I'm alright now and what's more, I'll buy you a pint." And never again did a harsh word pass between us and in 1956, after I had left the Lane, I heard that he was in hospital in a bad way with cancer so I wrote to him and received a letter that I and I hope the family will always treasure.

And now to Stratford where I moved to in January 1955. Here is a story or two about the great depot and its enormous district. Let us go to Wood Street, Walthamstow, where there is another shed working the Jazz similar to Enfield but the two little places are as different as chalk and cheese. Stratford was having a rough afternoon with failures and to cap it all, the running foreman had just been told that an N7 working up from Chingford with the usual two 'Quints' had come to a stand short of steam across the junction at Hackney Downs blocking three out of four of the running lines. It so happened that Bill Dixon, the Acting District Officer, and I were with the Running Foreman, Charlie Benton, at the time and when he heard that there was a certain very well-known Driver, George Seaborne of Wood St, involved. He told me to get off quick and have that man executed on the spot. So I slipped my 'revolver' into my pocket and away I went up to Liverpool St. Seaborne had not only arrived but he was attached to the next train to Chingford which showed no signs of getting underway. As I approached the engine, George spotted me and turned to his mate to say something about that interfering bastard, Hardy. However, I joined the two of them in the cab and said that it was time to go and the sooner the better. I had looked at the fire which was a huge misshapen mass and I said to George that I would be his fireman to Chingford. With a wicked glare, he replied with obvious delight that I would rue the day!

So away we went and George gave No 9620 nearly all she had through the tunnels under Bishopsgate, bursting out into the open whereupon he opened up still more but the harder he worked her, the better she steamed against the injector. As for me, I had nothing to do except to glance cheerfully at George with that mass of white hot fire working its magic. George ground his teeth and I laughed to myself. We stopped at James Street and then the lot to Chingford, the engine steaming perfectly and at Highams Park, I had a quick look at the fire, just a couple of small patches a bit thin and away we went again and ran up to Chingford. "Well, Guv'nor," said George as we shook hands, "you got the better of me this time!" And do you know that George Seaborne turned over a new leaf and in time he moved to Southend on the electrics and lived happily ever after.

LEFT: This picture shows the fork junction at Stratford. The main lines run up above as do the various branches and the carriage sidings. The L1 is near the end of her days but the low level lines under the main line station are very much alive. Likewise the tunnel although I doubt if it is used by men going home or taking duty these days. It used to save a lot of time! The photo shows the junction for Temple Mills via Chobham Farm and many other places but surely the low level tunnel and the station is still with us in more or less the same form. There is a similarity up above but nobody in those days including myself would ever have dreamed of the present truly great station.

LEFT: Here we have a B12 express passenger engine and a B17 fitted with the Westinghouse brake, the pump of which can be seen on the side of the smokebox. No 1601 was an Ipswich engine when I was shedmaster there from 1950–52. In the centre is the old 'Gobbler'. She is probably on her last legs but she will no doubt be working the usual service from Palace Gates to North Woolwich on this particular day. She is No 211 and has been at Stratford for many years. The Gobblers were well liked by enginemen, fitters and boilermakers; they were a simple engine, they could haul ten coach suburban trains when necessary and they were light on maintenance. When I came to Stratford in 1945, they were rostered to work the Enfield service with 14 stops and starts in ten and a half miles. Naturally the enginemen preferred the N7s, but they had plenty of life in them for the last two or three years of their existence. This photograph would have been taken in about 1956 and nobody realised that the Jubilee Shed would be a first class spotlessly clean diesel maintenance depot by the early 60s!

RIGHT: The cab of No 770 in August 1953 and the best I could do with a box camera. The low roof, round-topped firebox and high footplate combine to make the enginemen's world confined but not difficult to work in. The Driver is Sammy Gingell, wearing a beret, a rarity on the SR, but Sammy liked to cut a dash in a quiet way. His mate is Les Penfold and they must have been together two years in the Ramsgate link before Les moved over to the Brick in their dual link. A typical Eastleigh footplate with Drummond fittings. The firehole door goes back to Stroudley's days on the LB&SC and to the LSWR via Drummond, his works manager. The gauge glass protectors are unique to Eastleigh, with a spiked column on the right. It was said that LSWR firemen kept the water level with the top of the spike. Three steam valves in the centre are for steam heat, supplementary steam for the F class exhaust injector and for the sight feed lubricator behind Les's left shoulder. High up are the steam valves for the two injectors.

FAR TOP LEFT: No 123 Caley 7'0" single wheeler built by Neilson of Glasgow in 1886 to a Drummond design, preserved after its withdrawal in 1933. In September/October 1953, it came to Battersea Wharf for an exhibition. It was our responsibility and it was necessary to do some pretty heavy work on paint and above all steelwork. This was done by Johnny Millman, an ex-fireman who was labouring in the yard. It went back looking a picture and Johnny did a splendid job, for his generation did nearly 30 years of cleaning and firing. From the left: Jim McTague, Fitter and a Bulleid specialist, a great character from Inchicore, Dublin, with whom I kept in touch for many years; Assistant Foreman Fitter, Wal Thomas; Mr Wheeler, a visitor; RH; Fred Pankhurst, Chief Running Foreman; George Kerr ('Tick-Tock', always looking at his watch), Running Foreman; Johnny Millman, Shedman; Harry Newman, Acting Running Foreman; and Harry Biggs, Shed Engineman.

FAR BOTTOM LEFT: 1100 Victoria–Dover Boat Train hauled by rebuilt Bulleid Pacific. Driver Percy Tutt and his Fireman John Hewing made the day memorable for W O Bentley (in the cab)and myself. W O was a dear friend. He was a Doncaster Premium Apprentice in 1906, one of Mr Ivatt's pupils in 1910, leaving the service in 1911. Before the World War I, he and his brother had the concession for the DFP motor car and during the war, he designed the rotary engines, BR1 and BR2, fitted in the first case to the Sopwith Camel fighter in 1917. In 1919, Bentley Motors was formed and the rest is motoring history. I met him in 1958 and brought him back to the railway, his first love. This was his last trip on a steam engine. We had No 34101 Hartland and W O had a wonderful welcome from our crew. He sat on the fireman's seat and Percy gave me the regulator. We had a perfect journey to Dover, took the engine to the shed, prepared her and slipped across the line to the Archcliffe. We sat on our own in the back parlour and Percy and John, without realising it, got the normally reticent W O talking about his life with Bentley Motors – an hour to remember.

LEFT: Artful old 'Smithy' from Deptford and his 80-year-old steam crane standing near the softener sludge tank which is an old LB&SCR Stroudley tender. Here we have the sort of men who do not normally claim the spotlight and who deserve as much of a shedmaster's time as a main line driver or Grade 1 fitter or boilermaker.

From left: 'Con', whose Polish name nobody could pronounce or remember so he was Con, who worked as a shed labourer with Smithy and Frank Butowski; Tom Nightingale, Coalman, and I believe a bookie (although I did not know it at the time); Bill Price, Coalman (both men worked the mechanical coaling plant); Harry Keefe, Shed Driver; and Frank Butowski, strong and broad shouldered who liked and was worth overtime. If he didn't get it, he would swear in a comprehensive mixture of Cockney and Polish at the Chief Running Foreman who thought the world of him. He was one of the best and and if the crane 'broke down' he would make old Smithy work for a living with a shovel. Smithy was a likeable rascal who spoke very broad Cockney but in a thin, piping voice. We had to watch him but he was a real character.

TOP RIGHT: Taken in July 1957, the Sunday before Sammy Gingell's last week of service on the footplate, by Dick Riley, as the three of us had a part to play in the running of that remarkable shed, Stewarts Lane, Battersea. I had come across at Sam's request for what he called 'a little sprint' to Dover on the rebuilt No 34005. Sammy is on the right, a unique man who would take any engine on any train with any fireman. He had left school at 12 and had worked as a coalman's boy and then at about 14, he went off to South Wales to work down the pit as a haulier. He had his regular pony 'Cardiff' and he grew up to become the strongest of the strong with hands like boxing gloves. However, Sammy came home in 1913, got married and joined the SECR at Battersea as a cleaner aged 20. With many younger men ahead in seniority, he only had nine months in the Boat Train link but that didn't matter to him; he had done it all. On the left is the Chief Running Foreman, Fred Pankhurst, who was an ex-driver and had been a foreman down the Old Kent Road at Bricklayers Arms Shed. He was tough, illiterate and uncouth but he had a heart as big as a house and he saved thousands of minutes of potential lost time in finding men and engines to work the endless summer demands of the Traffic Department. He could cajole men to do the impossible, and how fortunate I was to have such support. A great shed with remarkable men who would take on anything and some of whom were 'good with a pencil' if they got the chance.

BOTTOM RIGHT: Nos 70004 and 70014, the *William Shakespeare* and the *Iron Duke*, are being prepared to work the *Golden Arrow* and, to use railway language, the second *Arrow* which left Victoria 30 minutes later at 2:30pm. There is nothing unusual about the photograph, but the fact that the cleaner, who is standing on the handrail cleaning the top of the smoke box, is in a dangerous position which was an everyday risk. Nobody was ever injured!

FAR RIGHT: October 1954. We had prepared No 34088 to go light to Eastleigh to return the next day from Portsmouth Harbour with the Emperor of Abyssinia, Haile Selassie, who would be met by the Queen and Sir Winston Churchill, the Prime Minister, at Victoria. I rarely had my camera at work but I took photographs that day, and here are two excellent Grade 2 fitters, with both of whom I had had high words in the past for we were all three independent and strong personalities.

Hatchets were always buried quickly at the Lane and here are Syd Walker and Wilf Price, the first a Cockney from outside the gate and the second from South Wales. We had some excellent fitting and boilermaking staff and had kept them after the war when craftsmen and semi-skilled staff tended to drift away unless they were dedicated to the job, as many were, although the pay wasn't up to much without overtime and weekend work. There were plenty of jobs for the semi-skilled men on a steam locomotive, especially on the Bulleid Pacifics. The electric lighting on the Pacifics was taken care of by the electric lighting department, which was not our responsibility.

ABOVE: No 768 about to leave the shed for the 3:35pm Victoria–Ramsgate, late 1954. My time at the Lane was running out and my little box camera was pressed into service for once. No 768 was always highly polished and well cleaned and she looked good. Here are four interesting people. From left: Jack May, now in No 2 link with Billy Reynolds – a splendid pair right up to the job. Jack had been the LDC Chairman and one of the best holders of the responsible position that I have ever met, straight, able, respected by all and able to see both sides of any issue. He was an NUR man elected for his ability by a largely ASLEF stronghold. He retired from the LDC in January 1954, still held in high regard, but never put himself forward again owing to the ASLEF strike in May 1955 when the NUR men ordered their men to work normally. Next, Freddy Burton, a Shed Driver with a big heart. He had been a top class fireman on the Nelsons before the war but after a while his eyes let him down and he was confined to shed limits. He was a lovely man, and so in his special way was Gerry McTague, Secretary of the Workshop Committee, on the right. He was a charming and persuasive Irishman from Inchicore, Dublin, and he and Bill Brooks were a very effective pair: they did a lot for the men they represented and made sure that my life was not one of slippered ease.

LEFT: In total 13 7MTs had been based at Stratford until January 1959, when I was obliged to transfer them all to Norwich due to our severe shortage of staff and the crippling onset of all aspects of diesel and electric training whilst maintaining our scheduled passenger and freight services, never mind the endless demand for engines and men for special working. At the end of steam in September 1962, some 60 steam locomotives were transferred elsewhere or withdrawn from service for good. The 'Human Revolution' in the huge Stratford District was complete.

ABOVE: A special Enfield–Hastings via Liverpool St and New Cross Gate and Lewes, ready to leave, through 'the Pipe' (East London tunnel) under the Thames. Two J69 'Buckjumpers', eight coaches, no condensing, made easy work for these strong little machines. Southern engine from New Cross Gate. On the left, 1,500 DC electric motor coach before conversion to AC traction.

LEFT: A Stratford B1, No 1280, on the 8:30am Liverpool St in September 1958 by arrangement, to give Mécanicien André Duteil of La Chapelle, Paris Nord, the experience of a Bongo on the down journey, and No 70036 with Driver Ted Whitehead on the return. Andre had had the Chapelon Pacific E4 as his own and then been promoted to the De Caso Baltics, his engine being No S002. He came three times to England as our guest and on the return journey in 1958, he drove No 70036 from Bentley, where we were booked to stop, as far as Shenfield. He always wore his cap back to front and with his SNCF goggles resembled (as Ted said) "The man from Mars."

This was Ted's last week in the Norwich gang before moving up to No 14, the L1 link, on outer suburban work. He was an outstanding driver, mate and 100 per cent for the railway. Andre never forgot Ted's kindness and his welcome – both spoke their own language yet understood each other! The 'Brotherhood of Railwaymen', of course!

RIGHT: Poster produced for BR to promote the Golden Arrow pullman day service to Paris, which operated daily from London Victoria. Artist unknown.

GOLDEN ARROW
PULLMAN DAY SERVICE TO PARIS

EVERY DAY OF THE YEAR FROM LONDON (VICTORIA)

SOUTHERN
BRITISH RAILWAYS

PUBLISHED BY THE SOUTHERN REGION OF BRITISH RAILWAYS 'AD707/A'| PRINTED IN GREAT BRITAIN BY M'CORQUODALE & Co. LTD., LONDON

ABOVE: Ramsgate train leaving Bromley South with driver Syd Frankham. This is No 1506, class E1, on her last summer at work. She is climbing the stiff 1 in 95 incline, master of the load but hard work. The coal in the tender is mixed with a lot of small stuff at the back, but her exhaust would be magnificent.

ABOVE RIGHT: The final touches to No 34088 before departure light to Eastleigh: prominent are the Royal buffers and the Royal drag hook and screw coupling. Next day the Royal brass beaded and polished disc boards will be set in the usual code for Royal trains. On the left is Bill Thorburn, an outstanding Chargeman Cleaner who worked extremely hard and led from the front. Chief Inspector Danny Knight on the right was in charge of the Inspectorate at T E Chrimes' HQ (MPS) at Waterloo and rode on all Royal or Deepdene duties.

RIGHT: Boxing Day 1954, my last week at Stewarts Lane. There are quite a few trains running including the *Golden Arrow*, engine No 34071, about to leave the shed at 12:35pm.

LEFT: Just before the evening peak, the Enfield N7 No 9665, embellished by its crew, leaves Liverpool St with a one Quint load. There are plenty of passengers and the fireman is well in control of the situation. He will be back again in Liverpool St with a ten coach loads each way before the peak eases.

BELOW LEFT: Back to Stratford and a typical turntable well positioned so that an engine can be turned at the same time as it is disposed and then straight down to the coaling plant. The ever-present 'Buckjumper' is vacuum fitted with the 'Westo' brake on the engine, both used for passenger work.

BELOW: We had three little P class 'Poppers', useful and strong little engines. I loved to see one pulling a heavy load of empty milk tanks from the Milk Depot down beyond Stewarts Lane Junction: no steam at the chimney-top however cold the day, and the exhaust was explosive!

ABOVE LEFT: The working of the Jazz out of Liverpool St to Enfield Town and Chingford in the peak hours was one of the wonders of the railway world. I have a photograph of Signalman B Alsford in vigorous action in Liverpool St Westside Box and below, thanks to David Butcher, railwayman and author, is a resumé of Alsford's duties during the evening peak in July 1946. "In his box, the signalman would continuously be operating the signals, points and block signalling instruments seeking clearance over the down suburban for each departing train and then 'Train entering section'. Alongside this he will be receiving and sending similar bell codes for trains coming to him on the up line. On average, every ten minutes, he worked something like 26 point lever movements, controlling some 40 individual sets of points, about 30 signal lever movements controlling 30 signals and 24 sent and received bell codes – some 80 actions or one every 7–8 seconds, in addition to which he had to keep a sharp lookout for anything untoward outside his box. He would maintain this work rate for some three hours with little respite. The Jazz was unique: occasionally I would look down from the Westside bridge and watch every move, great railway-work."

ABOVE RIGHT: The famous Pilots at Liverpool St. No 9614, west side: No 8619, east side. All brightwork was scoured and polished daily. Levelling pipes above the tank burnished for the first time by George Chittenden. Both engines stood ready to cover failures, No 9614 first choice, No 8619 station shunter.

RIGHT: Liverpool St Eastside platforms 11–18. From left: N7 with empty stock for Thornton Fields; B17 No 1647 on Ipswich line train; a Cambridge B1 No 1283 en route to the turntable and what looks like a standard 4MT. The train on the extreme right is a Southend No 1956 stock.

LEFT: The photographer is standing above the main stores and the water tank and looks down on a disposal pit where the Digger is loading ashes into wagons headed by a Buckjumper. On the right is the 'New Shed', actually built in 1871, which is used purely for the maintenance of engines. There is no ventilation so all engines in the shed are 'dead'. Three of the six roads in the shed can be seen; No 1 for diesel shunter maintenance, 2 and 3 used for rigorous examination on a time and mileage basis. Nos 4, 5 and 6 are out of sight. 4 and 5 being devoted to boilerwork and 6 for special examinations of engines with defects difficult to detect (plenty on steam locomotives) and preparation for special duties. In short, 6 had a very experienced staff who took on whatever came their way.

A variety of diesel shunters are standing in front of the shed, which would be hard at work on a weekday, and maintenance is always done on a Sunday. To the left with light-coloured doors is the Paint Shop, part of the Works, but Mr Gabbitas, the Foreman, was a good friend of ours. The blue East Side Pilot at Liverpool Street was thus painted in 1958 with the authentic GER blue, stored away these last 40 years. All the rest, except the buildings behind and beside the railway are Works property, No 2 Carriage Shop on the left but our Crane Shop is partially hidden by steam. Beyond and opposite to the foot-crossing are the MIC classrooms containing many sectioned locomotive components for the instruction of up and coming enginemen.

The Crane Shop Foreman is the legendary Breakdown Foreman Syd Casselton. He was brilliant in his use of the 36-ton crane and of the German re-railing equipment. His priority was to clear the main line as quickly as possible and, once started, Syd would brook no interference of any sort that would delay the resumption of traffic.

RIGHT: Poster produced in the 1950s for BR to promote the company's rail services. The style of the artwork makes a marked break from the typical poster art of the period, which was generally rather conservative. Artwork by B Myers.

BELOW LEFT: Stock poster produced for the SR showing the Bulleid Pacific locomotive travelling at speed along the tracks. Artwork is by Leslie Carr, who painted marine subjects and architectural and river scenes. He designed posters for SR, LNER and BR.

BELOW RIGHT: July 1953; a demonstration of the German Railing Equipment of which Stratford was the first depot to be so equipped. Bill Hunting, the Breakdown Foreman is at centre, while on the left is Sir Michael Barrington-Ward of the Railway Executive, a formidable figure who struck fear into many but never the bowler-hatted figure on the right, the great L P Parker, Motive Power Superintendent Eastern Region. By the time I came back to Stratford in 1955, L P Parker had retired and he died the following year, deeply mourned by hundreds of men who came to his funeral.

RIGHT: The back end from the Coaling Plant facing east. The J69 is shunting a raft of three tank engines to release No 7720. The J20 is fresh from general repair as is the B1. With endless marshalling and an enormous shed, foremen, shed turners and artisan staff have a job on.

SOUTHERN RAILWAY

ABOVE: From left: Running Foreman Bill Tindall, Chief Running Foreman Arthur Davey, and myself, Assistant DMPS Stratford. We are standing in front of No 90602 at the New (1871) shed, probably in 1957. The 350HP shunters and eventually the rest of the Stratford shunting fleet were maintained down Nos 1 and sometimes 2 road and the maintenance was of a high standard, because Ernie Button, the Chargehand Fitter had been dealing with these engines since 1944. What he and Les Thorn, who eventually became my Diesel Assistant in 1959, didn't know about those little machines would go on the back of a postage stamp. Arthur was one of the most energetic and dedicated of men, given to chewing pencils and humming to himself.

LEFT: Bishopsgate platform (station closed 1916): B17 4:00pm on up Yarmouth service. On the left are the up and down suburban lines in the tunnel. Above is Bishopsgate Goods depot and to the right is Shoreditch (Metropolitan) for the East London line.

ABOVE: Artwork showing advertising hoardings at a London station, circa 1962. Railway stations were a good place to advertise, as they would be seen by large numbers of people as they waited for their trains.

ABOVE: No 70039 is very much a Stratford engine coming up No 10 at Liverpool St at 1:55pm on the dot. She will stop under the hotel, quiet and smokeless. No 70040 is in No 9 with the 2:24pm Norwich via Cambridge. No 70039 had three great Drivers, Bill Shelley, Geo Warren and Ernie South.

RIGHT: Fred Smith (fourth on the left and clearly in charge) and his oil squad. Fred was the chargehand selected to organise the special arrangements at Stratford to counteract hot axle boxes and bearings on 350 steam locomotives. This was one of L P Parker's specialities and the arrangements were very satisfactory in reducing the number of over-heating bearings.

06

SNCF EXPERIENCE
ON NORD AND EST REGIONS

1958 —
1971

An invitation to travel on the famous Chapelon Pacifics from Calais to Paris could not be declined and it opened the door to the SNCF and its staff. How those French railwaymen loved visiting us and realised that we were not the unfriendly and reserved 'English' after all!

This is part of an article written in 1986 for a rather special book on France, its hotels and restaurants by Richard Binns and its title was *French Leave Favourites*. He asked me to compare the life of a SNCF steam driver and one recently charged with the working of the TGV service from Paris to Lyon. This is the first half, with some additions and minor changes, which describes a journey that I made on one of the great De Caso Baltics, the 232S003. The Mécanicien was André Duteil and his magnificent Chauffeur, René De Jonghe. The text is non-technical but one must say that the S003 was in its last weeks of service and that André's own S002 was already laid aside. These engines were stoker-fired and therefore the fire had to be maybe 6ins thick over the grate and the feed to the grate constant and directed to perfection. The coal was the size of small pebbles, perfect for stoker-firing and to get the hottest steam possible, the water was carried in the bottom nut of the gauge-glass throughout the journey with the utmost confidence. The temperature in the superheater was between 400° and 420° Centigrade which is very hot indeed.

"It is a warm summer evening in 1961 at Aulnoye in Northern France. Steam traction has nearly done on this section but tonight André, René and I are going to draw wonderful work from our old locomotive, the S3, which has but a month to go before being laid aside for ever. André, the mécanicien, is 5ft tall, a little gold-toothed, pink faced ball of fire of 48 who knew all about the Railway Resistance during the war, a marvellous driver, artistic in his use of the brake: René is one of the best of Firemen, tall, strong, quiet and immensely experienced. L'Equipe Duteil/De Jonghe come from the historic depot of La Chapelle, under the shadow of Montmartre. I know the road so André motions me to take charge of the locomotive. It is hot in the cab but when we are moving the wind will freshen us up although the fire will become blindingly white, requiring constant attention over the enormous grate; our faces will soon be black with coal dust and certainly the bucket of water hanging outside in the cool air containing bottles of citron will be needed for we shall have to think and work hard tonight.

"We are away with a huge packed train of 780 tonnes and the S3 soon gets into her stride. One does not need to press her with that load, but nevertheless, because we are late and time must be regained, we are going to reach our maximum permitted speed of 120kph quickly and then hold it, uphill and down-dale. This will need constant and careful adjustment of the controls and speed of firing, an intimate knowledge of the route, gradients and the position of the signals, for in the left-hand corner of the cab, under my only lookout window, lies the speed recorder which tells me everything I want to know but also charts the speed – *L' espion*, the spy! And how different from this country where one rarely if ever encountered a speedometer until near to the end of steam.

"And now the light has gone, a wall of blackness lies ahead of the long boiler for no headlights probe the darkness: stations flash by, Le Cateau, Busigny, one's head outside in the wind to pick up, as soon as they appear, the green signals that beckon us on, our old engine tearing into it, René in his element, for we are living parts of our machine which depends on the courage and skill of its crew. We are in a world of our own, cut off from authority, from our passengers, from every living soul except those in distant places who control the signals.

"We stop only once, at St Quentin, running up the long platform as fast as possible to save a few seconds, for every little counts. On again into the night, Tergnier, Noyon, Compiegne and then, as we approach the great junction near Creil, first yellow, then red lights bar the way but the road clears as we pass slowly through the station. We have lost some of the time we regained from Aulnoye, so now the S3 is opened out to shoulder her load, thundering up the long rise, spitting sparks of defiance high into the sky. On through Chantilly, over the viaducts, she gradually accelerates to 100kph, before we reach the summit near Survilliers, passing under 'Le Pont de Soupirs', momentarily illuminated by the open fire-hole door. And now our work is done, I hand over to André and we can spin silently, but ever vigilantly, down to Paris.

"As we climbed through Chantilly, Andre had served a good Bordeaux, brought specially for the occasion. Having uncorked, tasted and approved the wine, very much at room temperature, we drank to the great days of steam and to our own good fortune. At length, we drew quietly to a stand in the Gare du Nord. We have covered 134 miles in 132 minutes and, as we look down at the passing throng, we knew that we had reached the end of an era."

André and I had become firm friends after my first journey with him in April 1958 and since then he had visited the UK five times, sometimes to stay in London with James Colyer-Fergusson and to meet our railwaymen and travel on our engines. So many things were different: loose coupled freight trains were almost unheard of in France, engines without speedometers *encroyable* but the warmth of his reception was always unforgettable. I can see him now at Dover Marine running down the Invicta's gangway in his blue overalls, cap, scarf and goggles ahead of the passengers and then his typical Cockney reception on the Bulleid Pacific from Harry Wing and Peter Warner of the Lane.

RIGHT: What a picture of strength and control: March 1960 just before electrification to Amiens. Len Theobald, our Chief Locomotive Engine Inspector, who loved France and got on very well with the railwaymen, travelled back with me from Paris on Train 19 with the Calais men on E46. It was a wonderful journey and the engine was never worked hard despite a very heavy train. The Mécanicien was Henri Odent who was nearly 50 and on the verge of retirement, and his enormous Chauffeur, Robert Gourdin, in his later forties, seen here smoking a Gauloise, in far from vigorous action as he flicks the coal in the firebox with what appears to be a spoon in his formidable grasp. Apart from the back corners of the grate, the shovel hardly went near the door. The E46 looked a picture as can be seen overleaf, a credit to the work of both men as was the economy of coal. Incidentally the large brickettes can be seen stacked in the tender. Normally they are only used to build or rebuild the fire and a hammer blow breaks them in half as required. Excellent fuel when used for this purpose and roused up by the long poker when leaving a terminus.

LEFT: This is a wonderful Gallic silhouette: precision, concentration, left hand on straight air brake to get the exact speed of 15kph on the recorder for an emergency track repair. Remember that *L'espion* will have a record of his speed and that 9.2mph is very slow to be maintained over a distance on a locomotive with a heavy train on level track. The Conducteur is Amadee Gosnet from La Chapelle, one time Senateur Paris/Orléans who had been getting the very best out of his magnificent 16000BB, an electric locomotive which had to be driven – nothing boring about handling these machines. At first our driver did not quite know what to make of his English guests when we joined him at Amiens.

ABOVE: The Gare du Nord, Paris, March 1959: 231 E46, one of the last Chapelon Pacifics to be built in 1936/7 for the Nord, working the *Flèche d'Or*, train 19 to Calais. E46 was the *machine titulaire* of Mécanicien Henri Odent and his Chauffeur Robert Gourdin who were complete masters of the job. On the left is Philippe Leroy, the head of the Motive Power Deptartment on the Nord Region of the SNCF, a very dear friend, and when he retired in 1970, all his BR friends had him and Madame over to see them off in our warmest style. Alongside him is another old friend, Len Theobald, Chief Locomotive Engine Inspector under L P Parker.

ABOVE: It's 1960. While we were taking water, M Maire of La Villette (the Stratford of Paris) discovered that the left big-end was running warm and the Chief Inspector M Gabrion, who was riding with us (an Est Region regulation), is assisting him in dealing with the situation. Incidentally, the engine came off the train as booked at Bar-le-Duc and we took it back to Paris without further incident. The engine was a 241P, basically a PLM design modernised by André Chapelon, the only time that I have even seen one of the breed, and I was not particularly impressed.

ABOVE RIGHT: François Joly had the K73 from Amiens to Calais. We have just left Boulogne Tintelleries climbing up towards Wimereux, 1965. François has his hand on the wheel that controls the amount of high-pressure steam passing to the low-pressure cylinders. Below are the reversing gear and the small wheel which controls the degree of variation of the blast pipe orifice.

ABOVE: An early journey in 1961 with Henri Dutertre (right) and his BR cap but with his new Fireman, Arnaud Flament (left), who was champion billiard player of the SNCF Nord as well as becoming, after a couple of years with Henri, a firing instructor – in French *moniteur de chauffe*. Here he is with his bright eyes, and his tendency was at times to disagree with Henri. James Colyer-Ferguson, who died in January 2004, took me to France in 1958 and we returned many times. Henri was the first French engineman that we travelled with in April 1958, which was a remarkable experience; it also amazed the Frenchman that I was capable of firing the Chapelon Pacific, which I did from Amiens to Paris. It was the first of many weekends spent with James or the other BR railwaymen who came with me. We gave Henri a BR cap but the only way you could wear goggles that were provided on the SNCF was by reversing the cap so that the peak was at the back, much easier with the normal blue soft cap of the SNCF men.

LEFT: A classic, which includes me, René de Jong, André Duteil, George Mitchell and M Jean Kerleau, the Ingenieur en Chef at Aulnoye in 1961. I had been driving, and from the chimney of a stoker-fired engine comes a solid stream of fine gritty coal, so goggles were essential, as was a good wash but we had no time for that until we got to Calais via Lille! René was a magnificent fireman not far off retirement and he kept an unvarying boiler pressure and water level from start to finish, and anticipated every move necessary to achieve the perfect journey. George Mitchell was the Examining Inspector for the Eastern Region passing men for driving duties.

RIGHT: A happy photograph at Amiens in 1965. George Barlow (see overleaf) is on the right along with M Andre Corbier, the Chief Controller in the Amiens 'Permanance' (the Control at Amiens). George loved coming to France and that morning, with Train 16, he had had hold of the E9 for several sections and acquitted himself very well. The train was very heavy and it was necessary to have two engines, which was nonsense for the E9 could have handled 700 tons on her own without trouble, but towards the end the engines were treated gently!

From left: Henri Dutertre with his E9; Michel Rock, his fireman; the inimitable Raymond Lasquellac, 'Dunstable', who had a cousin living in Dunstable; and his mate Fernand Chaussoy, an *élève mécanicien*. This was the first time that I had met Raymond and his hilarious attempts to pronounce Dunstable (Doonstarb), St Albans (Sant Olbons) and Whipsnade (Vipsnard) were highly memorable. The man standing in the middle with scarf and hat is the Amiens Train Dispatching Foreman.

BELOW: This is Jacques Vidal the first time I travelled with him in 1961. We are not far off Vesoul, our speed drifting down and now was the time to take some pictures. We are going at 116kph on the *L' espion* and Jacques is a happy man for I had done the firing and much to his approval. There is no room in front of the driver for *L' espion* so it has to go over the other side and the mecru has to glance across to see that the speed is within the limit of 120kph on this stretch, although the Est, K, and Gs can run at 130kph, track permitting. As I write both Jacques and Jeannine Vidal are in their nineties and these last few years my two sons and I have regularly visited their home near Troyes. Each time Jacques has written and always says that the champagne will be on the table ready to drink at 11 o'clock sharp!

MIDDLE: George Barlow's favourite photograph, taken in 1967, of the SNCF visitors who he called 'The Old Firm', a title unknown today but often used for a group of soldiers, sailors or airmen who had served together and who were great comrades. George and Maurice Vasseur were two men completely at one with the other yet neither could speak a word of the other's language. But what an example this is of 'The Great Brotherhood of Railwaymen', the true membership of which transcends all boundaries of rank and position. Maurice was a Chapelon Pacific Mécanicien with 231E7, a Calais engine whose Chauffeur was Louis Sauvage. Louis had been a Boulogne fisherman who had joined the railway in his twenties and had been firing for many years on the fast trains between Calais and Paris. George was the engine driver in charge of the Romney, Hythe and Dymchurch Railway and had

his own engine, the *Green Goddess*, built in 1925, and he arranged a ride for his visitors. He had tried to join the LNER at Colwick, Nottingham, in 1934 as an engine cleaner en route to firing and driving but there had been no vacancies. He joined up early in the war and became a sergeant instructor for potential Royal Engineers drivers and firemen. Demobbed in 1946, he joined the Romney, Hythe and Dymchurch with whom he gradually became a legendary figure known all over the world.

BELOW RIGHT: Henri Dutertre and his last mate before the diesels came, p'tit Louis Lapierre (little Louis) who had fired for years on the E17 on the Paris jobs, a gentle giant whose shovel looked like a pencil in his enormous hands. They are running into Calais Ville with train 19 with the job well done (largely by me) and it is a splendid study of a happy *equipe*.

Their engine was 231G81 and they shared her with René Gauchet, both he and Henri top class men. As I write, Henri, a year older than me, is in pretty good form but his gigantic mate only lived a few years after retirement at 50. I met him once and he certainly wasn't the man he had been. But as a general rule, drivers and firemen on the SNCF retired at 50 and they could not they believe that ours used to be perfectly happy to carry on to 65 – indeed there were very sound reasons why they should do so if their health stood up. By contrast the French locomen started a new life and Henri, for example, has had all but 40 years of retirement. As I write I've had almost 33 years in retirement and I still love to go to railway gatherings to enjoy the company of men I worked with or heard of many years ago.

LEFT: 12 March 1966. Train 27 loaded to close on 650 tons has arrived at Boulogne Ville with a 141R of the later series with Box-pox coupled wheels and the Kylchap exhaust. These were thrilling, powerful machines, American design modified and greatly improved by Chapelon and used all over France. When this photo was taken, Henri Dutertre was sharing 231 G42 with René Gauchet, who has the engine that day. Henri has worked the 8:00am Calais Ville to Amiens, returning with train 27, after which the Calais boys took us out to dinner. On this occasion I had taken my dear friend Colin Morris who was still at King's Cross as Divisional Running and Maintenance Engineer. Despite his frequently sombre appearance, Colin was perhaps the most amusing man that I have ever worked with and also a very fine engineer and railwayman who was grossly underestimated by his seniors in the GN Line days. He and I had a perfect relationship both on the job and off it.

ABOVE LEFT: After arrival at Jeumont, our activities had included servicing the engine, walking heavy laden to the Jeumont messroom, a distinguished lunch with various wines, a walk across the Sambre Canal to an auberge for cognac and coffee and finally here we are resting as we wait for our train to arrive from Belgium. From left: Henri Douillet, the Senior Chauffeur at la Chapelle and normally Titulaire on the U1, André Duteil, author and James Colyer-Ferguson. We were, of course, in prime form despite our lethargic appearance. (See also overleaf.)

ABOVE: This is a lovely study of Edmond Godry and myself in 1969 outside the dormitory at Calais. Steam had not yet gone but the Pacifics had left Calais and the 66000 BB diesels were doing the job after a fashion but with no regularity. On this journey I had John Shone, a close friend from my Liverpool days, with me, and we had 141Rs to Boulogne, back to Calais, then passenger to Hazebrouck in an Autorail and back to Calais with Edmond as our guide. Our drivers were 'Dunstable' (Raymond Lasquellac), Roger Chabe, Champion Boule Player SNCF Nord who had been in charge of the 231K22, and Claud Scrieve who came on the scene too late to be a Pacific Mécanicien, a 'Senateur'.

ABOVE: In the messroom at Jeumont, 1962. We have had a marvellous lunch and will soon be ready for off after we have been across the Sambre for cognac and coffee. We have already prepared our engine for the return journey to Paris.

ABOVE RIGHT: Harry Noden, Carriage and Wagon (C&W) Assistant Liverpool St, and Arnaud Flament are enjoying themselves on the E9 between Amiens and Calais, Henri Dutertre, the driver, out of sight. On the left are (top) the control wheel for the ACFI feedwater heater. Below that is the lubricator for the pump and the handle protruding gives you a visual idea of how fast the pump is working. The wheel below is the water control for the right-hand live steam injector. Harry was a mechanical engineer who specialised in carriage and wagon maintenance and design. He came to work with us when the C&W department was merged with the Motive Power department as well as the Road Motor and Outdoor Machinery departments.

RIGHT: I was invited to represent BR on the last steam-hauled train from Paris Nord to Calais in May 1971. At Amiens, and having finished an excellent lunch en route, I was hailed by M Ravenet, the CME of the Nord and ordered to travel on the engine to Boulogne wearing my best suit. Getting up onto the K82, I found that M Leseigneur, the retired and legendary Chief Inspector of the Nord, was already there and in post-prandial form. He was immediately followed by Oscar Pardo and so we were six. But about two minutes before departure, a steward arrived and passed up three splendid steaks with all the trimmings and two bottles of vin rouge, side plate and glasses and a delicious pudding to follow. Left to right: M Josef Poissonnier (smiling as was his wont) and a colleague. M Phillipe Leroy, retired Motive Power Superintendent, Chef Mecanicien Edmond Godry, Mecanicien Jean Guelton and Chauffeur Michel Lacroix, all of Calais, the last of the 'Senateurs'. They had a great time eating a first class luncheon while I did the firing in my best suit!

07

TRAFFIC AND DIVISIONAL MANAGEMENT 1963–1973

By the end of 1962, departments had merged and I realised that I could tackle General Management. I was appointed Divisional Manager first to King's Cross and then to Liverpool. At both places we had a grand management team and we really did make things hum. Open meetings with the staff gave us great satisfaction.

After several months acting as locomotive engineer for the Eastern Region, it was decided that I might be capable of becoming a divisional manager but that I must have some experience before a decision could be made. So, in November 1963 I became the acting Traffic Manager at Lincoln, not without some qualms as I was new to Commercial matters and limited on Operating matters, although it was in my blood, whereas on the Running and Maintenance side, my main aim was to give Ken Taylor, the District Motive Power Superintendent, as much of a free hand and as much help as I had been given at Liverpool St by Harold Few.

And so it was that I found myself going to a distant meeting on a bitterly cold and windy evening, barely a fortnight after my arrival at Lincoln. My colleague, Derek Burton, was a very able railway officer but he would possibly admit that, in 1963, he was no expert at the mundane task of keeping his diary straight and his secretary had great difficulty in getting her chief to come to the point. It so happened that myself, Derek, and a young man called Frank Paterson, who was on the threshold of a splendid career, were on our way to Spalding by car to meet the Coal Trade (to me, a terrifying ordeal) on the contentious subject of coal concentration, whereby the railway delivered coal to a central point and the coal merchants had to come and get it, whereas in the past, they were delighted to use a full wagon of coal as a bunker on wheels on their local goods yard instead of it being used for another journey: Dr Beeching was dead right on this one as he was on so many others. On the way, Derek reminded me that he was meeting the Coal Traders of Boston the following week but somehow (and beyond his comprehension!) he was also billed to debate the closure of the railways of East Lincolnshire with a NUR Organiser, in public, at the roaring metropolis of Barton-on-Humber.

Derek had great charm, especially on such an occasion, and I found myself agreeing to stand in for him at Barton-on Humber without the slightest practical knowledge of the subject and over the coming weekend I tried to brief myself, although the more I learned, the less I seemed to know. On the day, Bill Boothright, our railway chauffeur, drove me through rain and sleet to arrive at Barton in what seemed to be total darkness. My spirit had sunk to an all-time low but my imagination was at full throttle for I could 'see' the hall, packed to bursting point with livid Bartonians, baying for the blood of the 'cretin' who was proposing to close their railway. I could 'hear' the jeers of derision and cat-calls as I made my faltering case whilst round after round of applause would no doubt greet the skilled invective of the NUR orator. I longed for the assurance of a Beeching, the charisma of a Fiennes, and the profound experience of a Johnson and, just now, I had none of these things. But I had asked Albert Bostock, the Grimsby sales assistant, to come along as part of the audience to bail me out and for this and many other things, I owe him a debt of gratitude.

However, it was 6:00pm when I arrived at the home of the gentleman who was going to chair the meeting. The welcome I received steadied my nerves and during dinner, my railway life came up for examination. When I mentioned the Southern and its amazing Bulleid Pacifics, a certain look, well known to me, came into my host's eyes and I knew that I was on a winner: a bargain was struck and in return for a nice little sprint to Bournemouth and back, he would see that I had a reasonable ride later on in the evening. Wine, good food and delightful company began to work its magic and when we arrived at the hall, I felt that I could take on the world. The world, however, proved to be not 300 infuriated Bartonians but some 20 pleasant and enthusiastic folk, most of whom were railwaymen of whom three were from the Guards LDC at Grimsby. The NUR organiser was a Docks man and the last thing he wanted was a public debate on a subject of which he knew about as much as I did. So we each said our piece and sat informally on the table answering questions, assisted, nobly, by Albert Bostock. It was a thoroughly enjoyable railway gathering in which the minute audience participated civilly and effectively and said they were glad to meet me! My baptism of fire was over and never again, however severe the opposition, was I to feel so lost and forlorn, although I had still to learn many lessons on the importance of preparation and the dangers of extemporising in public. And as a matter of interest, Barton-on-Humber still has its railway!

The life of a divisional manager was endlessly interesting, enjoyable, difficult and challenging. Above all, in my sort of division, I dealt with people, the most fascinating study of all. My last division was Liverpool, where I dare to say that I was well known and respected by our huge staff and I had a first-class management team who were truly worthy of the name. But although we did a first rate job and achieved many economies, I was not a 'bottom line' man and therefore seen by the new top brass as no longer worthy of promotion in General Management with a big reorganisation pending that was to eliminate the divisions so let us confine ourselves to people in these few words in the King's Cross and Liverpool Divisions.

At King's Cross, Reg Clay, a wise and experienced Staff Officer who had started on the GC in 1917 as a boy messenger put it to me that we ought to re-start the informal communication meetings with our staff so that they should know what lay ahead that would affect their lives: these meetings had foundered during my predecessor's time. We did start to the tune of three meetings covering the division every six months and, knowing how my predecessor had fared, I dreaded the first meeting for the audience would contain the sardonic and able Charlie

TOP LEFT: Burgh-le-Marsh on the East Lincs below Willoughby, 1964. Bert Webster and Harry Amos admire the work of the proud station Foreman. Bert had been my assistant and true colleague when I had been at Liverpool St. When he joined me, I was 35 and he was 57 and we balanced each other perfectly. He had retired when he visited us at Lincoln and greatly enjoyed his day out with Harry and myself judging stations and seeing a part of the railway unknown to him.

TOP RIGHT: These were some of my right-hand men during my short stay of seven months at Lincoln preparing the district to enter (against its wishes) the new Doncaster Division in June 1964. From left: Ernest Needham, Chief Clerk, Harry Amos, District Operating Superintendent, and Jack Luty, District Traffic Inspector. There was a degree of comfort in the old coach and it served us well; always known as the 'Special'.

BOTTOM LEFT: The 'Special.' A GN body and frames on Gresley bogies? Anyhow, the old coach rode very well and enabled me to see much of the district in a short time.

BOTTOM RIGHT: Preparation for an Eastern Region Board visit is bad enough but when they are accompanied by two ferocious BRB members, Philip Shirley and Fred Margetts, men wanted to put up the shutters. So one goes over the route beforehand. We are at Collingham and the Board arrived from High Marnham (where I joined them) and we came in to Lincoln via Skellingthorpe and Pyewipe. The Central Station Master, Mr Chadwick, and I successfully weathered a Shirley inquisition. Then to St Marks via the East Yard where Shirley pinioned me in a corner with the unanswerable question: "Why have you got two stations at Lincoln, Hardy? Get one closed at once." Our engine is a B1 No 1406 with our inspection coach and, from left: Station Master Collingham, Jack Luty, Harry Amos, Derek Burton, Norman Micklethwaite, Sheila Hazard, my secretary, Ernest Needham, Bill Boothright, with three enginemen behind and a goods guard.

TOP: The Castle class No 7029 had just arrived at Peterborough for a month's work in the hands of New England men who did very well and enjoyed themselves. The year is 1967 and John Betjeman looks down in the classic pose of the old GWR drivers and behind him stand Reggie Hanks and, beyond, Horace Botterill, Foreman Fitter of vast GN and LNER experience.

BOTTOM LEFT: In March 1968 Burton men were working a train of fly ash from Drakelow Power Station to the Fletton Brick Pits. The driver did not know the road beyond Stamford and picked up a conductor at Toton. As they moved up slowly, Aubrey Dolman, who was the Burton Driver's Mate, shouted that there was a red light ahead, but the driver took no notice and, seconds later, they ran into another fly-ash train: both drivers were killed instantly and Aubrey was trapped and unable to move.

The breakdown cranes from New England and Finsbury Park were in position and the rescue men hard at it by the time I arrived to join Colin Morris. The problem was the impossibility of using burning tackle to free Aubrey, and a heavy wagon was entangled with what was left of the cab, a menace to the life of the trapped man. By 4:00am two alternatives were left: the amputation of a limb and the end of a driver's career as an engineman, or a grave risk to be taken involving the use of two cranes to make a lift of a few inches under great stress. All I had to do was to take a decision without hesitation. This risk was taken with delicacy and precision, a way was created, and Aubrey was borne away to hospital. He had smoked his pipe and talked to his rescuers, and had the courtesy to thank us all.

BOTTOM RIGHT: The group shows us from left: Colin Morris, Divisional Running and Maintenance Engineer, King's Cross; John Betjeman; Edwin Howell, Divisional Movements Manager; the great W O Bentley and myself at Wansford, which was then in my King's Cross Division.

Evans, Goods Checker, and the explosive Bert Goldfinch, who represented the cartage staff at King's Cross Goods, not to mention the smiling, conversational and very shrewd Steve Watts, as was that legendary veteran of many a Top Shed battle, Driver Bob Lunniss. In fact the meeting of over a hundred men was tough, hard hitting and humorous, yet correct. One was given an extra strength to handle the meeting and wonderful support from my management support. We kept this going and told the staff that I had attended a meeting with the BRB which proposed the closure of King's Cross station and for the concentration to be on St Pancras. At my last meeting before I left for Liverpool, I was able to tell the gathering that the plans had proved unworkable – to prolonged cheering!

And so to Liverpool, a new world far away from the Euston HQ, which was respected when that masterly GM, Bobbie Lawrence, was in charge. He let us get on with the job but he had us all nicely taped. So I started the same but renamed review meetings, which were most successful and enjoyed by many of those who came, for one of the great advantages was that people met each other informally before and after a meeting who would otherwise never have crossed paths. But there were moments: at my first meeting with the staff of the Area Managers Birkenhead, Northwich and Ellesmere Port, relief signalman Raymond Dickey of Hooton rose both to his feet and to the occasion. Never had I had such a lambasting as the blood rose up his neck and he became scarlet with indignation as he informed me that he had no love for divisional managers and little respect for them. I kept my temper and, in time, gained his respect and when I left in September 1973, he brought me a little gift that I shall always treasure. I loved those meetings in the Liverpool Division and they served their basic purpose of drawing management and staff closer together. And they were usually humorous!

Except for one at Garston. A certain very senior BR officer was visiting the Division to 'meet the chaps', so we called a day-and-a-half of meetings in which he insisted on being Chairman. I introduced him at every meeting and then, rightly, took a back seat. Question-and-answer was going well when a Garston driver who had asked the first question (he usually did), and been well satisfied with the reply, rose to raise some other issue. The Chairman was going strong with the reply when the questioner thought he had got it wrong and interrupted him, whereupon the Chairman shouted at him: "Will you bloody well shut up and listen?" That was the end of the meeting: the audience broke up and walked out; they simply would not have that sort of behaviour from the railway's top man. It was second nature to me to deal with such an interruption and, "Just hang on a minute and let me finish", would have had that audience of hard-bitten railwaymen in the palm of his hand.

ABOVE: Euston about 1987. In the centre is Jack Cherry, a much-loved GP in Abingdon who was going with me to Liverpool for the first time and also to watch Liverpool play at Anfield – a rugger man through and through! For a short time, the London jobs were manned because of the mileage limitation by two drivers out of the top link, and here are Arthur Owen and Tommy Perkins, both Scouse comedians, to entertain Jack and to educate him in railwaywork for both were able men. On arrival and after introductions, Jack climbed into the cab to be greeted with, "Now you're here, Dochter Sherr-ie, wah about a free consultation?" What a happy journey it was too and the return journey was the day of the Bushey disaster so Jack saw railway work in the raw on the way home.

ABOVE RIGHT: I was Divisional Manager Liverpool from May 1968 to September 1973, the experience of a lifetime. We took our Saloon, which we shared with the District Engineer, out on working inspections, which were hard but necessary and enjoyable. This is August 1973, my last outing before leaving the Division and we are at Delamere CLC when the station had a signalbox and a species of yard. From left (standing): Arthur Williams, my deputy and a truly good one; the incomparable Danny Whelan, Operating Superintendent; Arthur Behrend, who lived near our Wirral village of Burton; Ken Lord, Maintenance Engineer, who had been reared on the Southport electrics and later on the MS&W section; Roland Lancaster, the first commuter to rumble me (the service was so bad from Chester to Rock Ferry that I did not disclose my hand at once); Denis O'Reilly, Area Manager, Northwich, once S M Mullingar, very Irish and a really good railwayman; Jack Appleby, pillar of the Mail Room and excellent relief Steward; Peter Summers of JS&S, now part of BSC, dedicated to steel-making and a good friend; Jack Berry, our Guard and Inspector for the day and Fred Lancaster, a farmer and brother of Roland. From left (front): Alan Newitt, at Edge Hill in the 'Extra' link; John Connolly, our much-loved Steward; George Bordessa, Driver, once of Edge Hill and presently at Garston depot; and finally the remarkable Reg Holmes, Delamere Signalman and character.

ABOVE LEFT AND RIGHT : On 11 August 1968 a special train was run from Liverpool Lime St to Carlisle via Manchester to celebrate the end of steam traction on British Railways. I travelled on the Black 5 No 45110 to Manchester, and the photograph shows the Deputy Mayor of Liverpool and his daughter in the driving seat, and Driver John Hart, a 1924 man who must have done over 20 years' firing and completed 46 years' service. Brian Bradley, his Fireman, would have been passed for driving shortly afterwards. The Chief Inspector of the LM Region, John Hughes, was in overall charge and he was amazed at my request (as a newly appointed Divisional Manager) to put a few rounds on the fire during the journey. In the evening I went to Lime St to welcome the train home and here I am with Fred Smith, also a 1924 man, and his Fireman Steve Roberts. Like the morning men, they came from what was left of Edge Hill depot, a shed with a great reputation for fast running and variety of work. I was just beginning my time at Liverpool and I knew even then that I was going to enjoy the Scousers, although whether they would admire me was another matter!

ABOVE: For the time that Driver Fred Griffin had her along with Charlie Rolstone and Charlie Sampher, No 70037 *Hereward the Wake* was kept as in the photograph, a joy to behold. Much work was done by the enginemen themselves, as well as the cleaners, and like all our 7MTs she was a splendid engine at her work. 70037 is standing at Cambridge waiting to return to London with a special train and 'Griff' and his mate have been hard at work: the cab would be sparkling and all steel, brass and copperwork re-polished yet again. Fred wears his uniform cap with the GER Bat's Wing above the peak, overalls clean on every day, highly polished boots, but there was nothing fancy about him; he simply loved and had pride in his work. He knew, too, that his time would eventually be up in the Norwich link and then he became an early diesel instructor. He also brought the first 1250hp Brush diesel into Stratford Works in October 1957. His son Laurence was a Driver for Enfield in charge, along with two other sets of men, of the beautifully kept N7 No 9665. Regular manning was the main reason that in the last week before electrification in November 1960, not a minute was booked against any engine working the Jazz services from Liverpool St to Enfield and Chingford. Steam really did go out in a blaze of glory on the Jazz, where, in the peak, there was a steam-hauled train climbing Bethnal Green bank every two-and-a-half minutes.

ABOVE LEFT: Car being loaded onto a British Railways Eastern Region train. This train transported both passengers and their cars, allowing people to go on holiday by train but still take their cars. This service began in 1955 between King's Cross and Perth and proved to be successful.

ABOVE RIGHT: Signalmen at work in the interior of the Willesden signal box, North London, during the British Transport Films production *Willesden Signal Box* made in April 1966. How things have changed.

THE YEARS BEFORE AND AFTER RETIREMENT 1973 ONWARDS 08

By 1973, I was nearly 50, DMs were to disappear and I came up to the BRB at Marylebone to a job that I grew to love, a job in the making and the perfect job from which to retire at the peak. So, with that very useful financial inducement, I retired at 59 and life has been truly full and happy.

In October 1973, Gwenda and I left Liverpool and our home in Wirral with a heavy heart. I knew that my career was at the crossroads and that I should not realise my ambitions in General Management. It hurt at the time but I knew in my heart that it was the right decision. Initially I was responsible for the career development of all professional engineers in the Mechanical and Electrical and the Signal and Telecommunication as well as in the main workshops (British Rail Engineering Ltd) from their recruitment up to a level where their careers could be encompassed by the BR Management Development organisation. But I had the priceless advantage right from the start that I reported to the Chief Engineers and not to the Director of Personnel. When I left Liverpool, there were 5,690 people in my Division whereas in my new job, I had a lady clerk, Mavis, and Janet, my secretary, skilled in shorthand, and we worked hard and moved mountains in the end. Mavis retired just before me, Janet got married and was replaced by Margaret, and what a happy little team we were. I was involved, if I so wished, in every engineering appointment up to a certain level and I am glad to say that my previous career had prepared me well for what my job eventually became.

As my responsibilities widened so did my influence but only because I managed to overcome the stranglehold of red tape by cutting it but never forgetting to tie it up again after the job was done. Up to 1975, the proud and independent Department of the Chief Civil Engineer wanted no truck with me but then, the defences were lowered and I began to get to know as many of the younger men in training and well into their careers as possible. I loved working with the Civils, and their Regional Chiefs were glad to take advantage of my experience. I had worked closely with Civil Engineers especially at District and Divisional Level.

By and by, I became involved with the top management grades and then finally with senior officers. By this time my own staff had been increased by another clerk, Linzi, to help Mavis, but by about 1979 I was advising the Director of Engineering as well as the chief engineers on appointments and they generally took my advice which did me a power of good. Of course the Divisional Managers had engineering managers, most of whom were on my lists and what a joy it was to rescue an able man from a dead end or working for the wrong man and then manoeuvre him into the right position working under the right man. I remember my Director disagreeing with my recommendation of an engineer to fill a very senior post. I told him his choice was the wrong one and he took my advice after I had stuck to my guns and appointed the hardened fighter that was the right choice under the circumstances.

Not always as rewarding as that but in the main, a marvellous job with a great deal of influence; a sense of humour was vital, as was a certain strength of purpose. I had made a recommendation to a certain Divisional Manager and he appointed someone else by no means suitable. I knew the reasons and it was no surprise to me to hear that he had told Dick Hardy to "get stuffed". Two years later, I found myself in a similar situation and I took a chance and strongly recommended a good man but by no means the right one. My old colleague fell for it and appointed the right man for the job whom I wanted but had not recommended. A chance but it came off and both of us were happy for different reasons and the old boy never knew he had been conned!

The photograph on page 178 shows Alf Murray clipping the ticket of a lady passenger. Alf had been a driver at the Lane, the first man to whom I spoke to ask the way to the office of the DMPS who was going to brief me about my new job. He was a remarkable and a truly good man who had started at Battersea in 1917 and, in my time, was in No 5 link, the Chatham goods link that had a great deal of passenger work in the summer. When he retired from the footplate, he started a second career at Ashtead where he lived as a railwayman with responsibility for the car parks and many other duties. All the passengers liked and respected him and his knowledge of the railway, train times and what was likely to happen when things went wrong. He knew most of the drivers on the electrics as after steam was finished at the Lane, he had transferred first to become a motorman at Leatherhead and then to Dorking North. So he knew the form and stayed in that job until he retired a second time when he was 80. He was a real railwayman, an engineman, a good ASLEF man and he appreciated a management that got things done. He lived until he was 94 and I went to his funeral as did many other men from the Lane, one of whom was Percy Abeydeera. This is a letter that he left for me when I left the Lane which I treasure.

Dear Sir
It is with regret that I learned that you were leaving us so soon. Without any fear of contradiction I can honestly say that Stewarts Lane has benefitted by your short period of Shedmaster.
An official who can demonstrate with his own hands how a job should be done gains the respect if not admiration of all thinking footplate men.
For what you have done and tried to do at our Depot during your stay the majority of us I am sure are grateful.

Yours respectfully
Driver A Murray

RIGHT: Appleby and most of Julian Riddick's normal team back in the early 1980s. His A4 No 4498 named *Sir Nigel Gresley* is in the yard at Appleby, having worked from Carlisle and would work forward to Hellifield where the train reversed and was worked round to Carnforth, Lancaster and Preston. A perfect trip, although Julian was at the throttle part of the way and he was a rough handful when he was performing. The A4 crowd were first class as were the greater part of those in charge of the various steam locomotives in those days. Some such as Tom Tighe, a real Yorkshireman, are still hard at it and here you have the 'Gresley' and they were a pleasure to work with. From left: Robert Riddick, Terry Wheland, Julian Riddick, John Graham, Norman Hugill, George Gordon, Chief Loco Inspector at Carlisle on his last steam trip before he retired, Eddie Gibbons, Ian Howson (head next to nameboard), BR driver, firing for the day, Davie Hine, Driver, the PW ganger at Appleby, Ben Hervey-Bathurst, and my guest with me about to work my passage. Julian was a dear force to be reckoned with: it was he as much as anybody who put me up for election as Chairman of SLOA (Steam Locomotive Operators Association), a task that I greatly enjoyed. Julian loved to ring me up at 11:00pm and sound off about some supposed injustice and try to enlist my support. He usually had his way, but if not, he would tell me that I was "a bloody bureaucrat," and a few minutes later, "Well, goodnight, old chap, you always do your best for us". I had the honour of speaking at his funeral.

LEFT: Here we have Don Dutton, Jack Beaman, John Robinson ('Robbo') and myself together with the LNER K4 No 3442 *The Great Marquess* in apple green livery, based in 1999 on the Severn Valley Railway (SVR), in perfect condition in every department. To have a day with these three splendid railwaymen was an annual event. From left: Don Dutton, a volunteer who spent many happy hours on the footplate as John Robinson's fireman as well as days in the workshop; then Jack Beaman, still on BR as a Saltley driver and the Chief Loco Inspector of the SVR. I am between Jack and John; John was the mechanical foreman at Bridgnorth and had a driving turn from time to time. I was very much at home on this LNER engine, except that No 3442 lifted her safety valves for she would steam on a candle. In March 2010, back on the SVR, she was a very different engine and never got near to lifting them. I realise now that the Scottish fireman who was present seemed rather keen for me to have a go, which of course I did but with minimal success: later we found out how much dirt there was on the firebars.

RIGHT: The 'Rocket' with Bold Cooling Towers in the background in 1980. From left: Jimmy Donnelly, then the senior passed fireman at Edge Hill, Captain Bill Smith, the owner of the old GNR No 1247, J52; Peter Hardy, out for the day; Fred Dale ('The Principle Boy'); and Wilf Hulme, next in seniority to Fred.

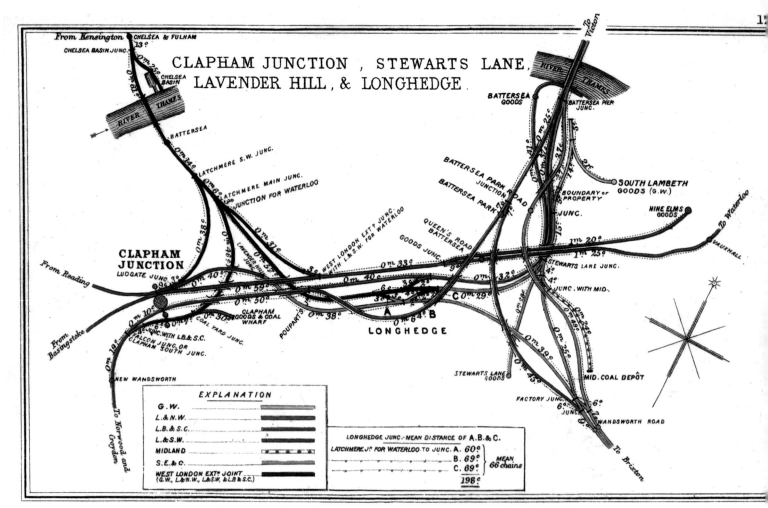

CLAPHAM JUNCTION , STEWARTS LANE, LAVENDER HILL, & LONGHEDGE.

From Kensington CHELSEA & FULHAM

CHELSEA BASIN JUNC.

CHELSEA BASIN

RIVER THAMES

BATTERSEA

LATCHMERE S.W. JUNC.

LATCHMERE MAIN JUNC.

JUNCTION FOR WATERLOO

CLAPHAM JUNCTION

LUDGATE JUNC.

From Reading

From Basingstoke

COAL YARD JUNC.

JUNC. WITH LB.& S.C.

FALCON JUNC. OR CLAPHAM SOUTH JUNC.

NEW WANDSWORTH

To Norwood and Croydon

CLAPHAM GOODS & COAL WHARF

POUPART'S

LAVENDER HILL JUNC.

WEST LONDON EXTⁿ JUNC. WITH L.&S.W. FOR WATERLOO

QUEEN'S ROAD BATTERSEA GOODS JUNC.

A

B

LONGHEDGE

C

BATTERSEA PARK ROAD JUNCTION

BATTERSEA PARK

BATTERSEA GOODS

RIVER THAMES

To Victoria

BATTERSEA PIER JUNC.

BOUNDARY OF PROPERTY

JUNC.

SOUTH LAMBETH GOODS (G.W.)

NINE ELMS GOODS

To Waterloo

VAUXHALL

STEWARTS LANE JUNC.

JUNC. WITH MID.

To Brixton

STEWARTS LANE GOODS

MID. COAL DEPOT

FACTORY JUNC.

JUNC.

WANDSWORTH ROAD

EXPLANATION

G.W.
L.&N.W.
L.B.& S.C.
L.&S.W.
MIDLAND
S.E.& C.
WEST LONDON EXTⁿ JOINT
(G.W., L.&N.W., L.&S.W., &LB.&S.C.)

LONGHEDGE JUNC.- MEAN DISTANCE OF A.B.& C.
LATCHMERE Jⁿ. FOR WATERLOO TO JUNC. A. 60°
                                          B. 69°   MEAN
                                          C. 69°   66 chains
                                          198°

ABOVE: A 1912 Railway Clearing House map of the lines around Stewarts Lane. The British Railway Clearing House was an organisation set up in 1842 to manage the allocation of the revenue collected by railway companies for fares and charges paid, for passengers and goods travelling over the lines of other companies. It produced Railway Junction Diagrams (RJDs) which were extremely accurate.

RIGHT: In the cab of a diesel shunter whilst enjoying a naming ceremony, hosted by Southern General Manager Gordon Pettit at Stewarts Lane.

BELOW: Stewarts Lane depot, Christmas 1991. Stewarts Lane was a large railway servicing facility in Battersea, London, founded by the London Chatham and Dover Railway (LCDR) in 1862, to serve London Victoria railway station. It was sited in the midst of a maze of railway lines between 'Factory Junction' and 'Stewarts Lane Junction', adjacent to the site of the former Longhedge Railway Works. Today it is used as the depot for the Gatwick Express.

LEFT: Clipping a lady's ticket at the barrier is Alf Murray. When the photograph was taken he was a day or two short of his 80th birthday and he lived until he was 94. Bombed out twice during the war, he was evacuated to Leatherhead, which by coincidence was where I was born. He was a splendid driver and much liked by everybody, helped his comrades whenever he could, and as far as I was concerned, it was a joy to work with him. He had started in 1917 and become a fireman in the Nelsons before the war: his Nelson had the Lemaitre blast-pipe fitted and Alf always said she was a flyer. He did great work as a passed fireman getting driving turns during the war and especially in the air raids. When I was Divisional Manager at King's Cross, I sometimes travelled to Surbiton with him and enjoyed driving and above all stopping with the old Queen Mary stock. When he reached 65, he had already been an electric train driver some years based at Dorking and as he lived in Ashtead, he applied for a railman's position at the station. He became the passenger's friend, looked after the car park, helped people who were in difficulties over travel arrangements. He loved his work for he was well known by all the Western Section motormen, some of which had started at Stewarts Lane and had even fired for him.

RIGHT: Annually, the Cambridge University Railway Club was given an E4 No 2785 – the last to survive. BR provided two coaches, a driver, a fireman, and inspector to give the young people instruction in driving and firing. Here she is entering Bartlow with an undergraduate at the regulator (if not the brake). A great event.

LEFT: Here is my friend 'Blanche' (along with the 'Linda') at Boston Lodge and against her stand a good cross section of the Locomotive Department, both permanent staff and volunteers. I had 10 years on the Ffestiniog Railway Company Board from 1977–87, an unforgettable and bracing experience and by no means an easy ride. So here we go.

From left: Clive Gibbard; Colin Dukes, son of Paul Dukes, who served the railway as Locomotive Engineer for many years; Paul Ingham, with whom I paired up for four days each year as his fireman. Then comes Alwyn Jones, a volunteer of many years standing, as was Jo Clulow behind him and whose father was one of the Company's doctors. Jo gave a great deal of time to the railway, not only on the engines but on the Operating side and in the Control. Then John Davis and Colin Sudland, who were both volunteers at Boston Lodge; the little chap next to him is 'Shadwell', who was a Welshman with very Welsh names, which defeated many of the English staff, Llyn Aploto, so he was known instead as 'Shadwell'. Then comes Roy Harper, a volunteer at the Lodge, and finally Andrew Arrowsmith who was known as 'Arry, which went well with his surname.

RIGHT: Between Sunday, 31 March and 6 April 1985, the replica Gooch 8ft Broad Gauge Single Wheeler paraded on a straight stretch of track in Hyde Park near the Royal Albert Hall and she was named the 'Iron Duke' by the Duke of Wellington on 3 April. I was co-opted by Major Olver of the Railway Inspectorate to pass out drivers from the Kent and East Sussex Railway and I recruited Bert Hooker ex Nine Elms to train the drivers while I passed them out. What a sensation that huge engine with its enormous chimney must have created in 1851 when she could spin along with a light load at 70mph but she had no brake on the engine, only on the tender. (How did you stop in those days? You reversed the engine and gave her steam, an unofficial practice that survived to the end!) From left: Mike Hart, Managing Director of Resco who built her; Tony Hall-Patch stands on the step wearing his old Royal Engineers cap; then Bert Hooker and John Higgins who, along with John Sinclair and others, actually built the engine.

ABOVE: The Ravenglass and Eskdale Railway in Cumbria runs through marvellous Lakeland countryside and up into the hills. After her marriage, our daughter lived at High Saltcoats and my wife and I went to see them every so-often. But I had also travelled on No 4472, *Flying Scotsman*, previously from Carnforth to Ravenglass and the fireman was by no means a youngster. He knew that I was a railwayman as the Inspector Bert Moore had been tipped off but was surprised when I offered my services. He looked very doubtful but agreed that I should try a round or two. I had first fired a Gresley Pacific in late 1941, nearly 40 years before.

ABOVE: My collection of photographs is held by Barry Hoper at Transport Treasury. He operates out of Insch, Aberdeenshire, and once a year I make a trip up there to help him with the archiving of the photographs. This image is of me on the nearby Keith and Dufftown Railway. This is a Class 108 DMU, No 56224.

LEFT: 1 May 1993 and Bryan Gibson and I are in charge of the LMS Ivatt Mogul No 46441 belonging to the Beet family, who enjoyed the splendid working of this grand little engine over what was once the Met & GC section. We have come up from Harrow-on-the-Hill to Amersham and everything was just as it should be up the 1 in 105 up to Amersham. We worked 50:50 driving and firing, just like the old days and on the first round, we had two distinguished visitors on the footplate, one being Ian Arthurton who was then General Manager of Underground and the other, none other than Derrick Fullick, General Secretary of ASLEF and an old Nine Elms man just down the Wandsworth Road. ASLEF was the Union to which Bryan belonged in his BR days at Holbeck, Leeds. It was my turn at the regulator so I told Derrick to take her to Rickmansworth, which he did without batting an eyelid. We had six bogies and were dragging *Sarah Siddons*, no need for her assistance for our little engine was very much in charge. As for Bryan and I, we were in our element for he was an old LMS engineman (not his fault) when I was at Stewarts Lane depot and we had a few of the tank engine versions of our little class 2.

LEFT: Myself and Michael Kerry, who was my oldest friend and who died about five years ago. He became Sir Michael with a distinguished legal career but he never lost his lovely temperament, and his interest in railways and railwaymen never waned. One day, an engine-driver friend was quizzing us on engines. Looking at me, he said, "What is a vacuum?" I did my best to explain but soon got nowhere fast. A glance at Michael, whose reply could not be bettered: "Nothing."

We are having a memorable day on the Bluebell Railway with Gerald Butler and Sam Bee, his Fireman, taking it easy. Michael was a good Driver and improving with his use of the brake as the day wore on. His Stoker (me!) enjoyed himself firing for his oldest friend!

ABOVE: The Keighley and Worth Railway played host to some 40 former Southern Region footplate crews and their partners on Monday 23 February 2015 , when we were able to renew acquaintances with an old friend, an unmodified Bulleid Pacific in the shape of No 34092 *City of Wells*. I was one of the visitors as I was No 34092's shedmaster at Stewarts Lane, Battersea when she was operating the *Golden Arrow*.

We rediscovered old skills as our four coach train made four round trips over the branch. The recent heavy rain relented to give a clear, crisp day and test No 34092's ability to keep the train warm. Many reminiscences were shared and a wonderful day was had by all.

ABOVE LEFT AND RIGHT: Much of this book is about personalities and I am thankful that my career included working with so many railwaymen, literally thousands of them. One still sees them as if they were alive and as full of character as ever, and for that reason I am putting them at the end of the book long after our time together, for I feel that they will bring back the atmosphere of those days long past. The photographs were taken in 1963 by Driver Jack Searle and he gave me about 20 pictures of different men, mostly taken after I left the District. Here are Albert Page and Ted Whitehead, both 7MT men, Albert on No 70001 and Ted on No 70036, both engines well cleaned and all copper, brass and steelwork beautifully burnished, their nominated engine in which they took great pride.

RIGHT: 27 July 1986 between Warwick and Banbury, Driver Vic Waites and 'The Old Stoker' then a mere 63 years old flicking the coal into the back right-hand corner of the grate. It was very important to keep the back corners replenished. There is plenty of heat in this fire and I'm wearing a glove to protect myself. Tea cans are on the tray. Vic has the regulator well open and is driving with a short cut-off, and economically. This is what this old engine likes — No 4498 class A4 *Sir Nigel Gresley*, one of the best.

INDEX